THE
PARENT
YOU WANT TO BE

Resources by Les and Leslie Parrott

Books

51 Creative Ideas for Marriage Mentors
Becoming Soul Mates
The Complete Guide to Marriage Mentoring
Getting Ready for the Wedding
I Love You More (and workbooks)
Just the Two of Us
Love Is . . .
The Love List
Love Talk (and workbooks)
The Marriage Mentor Training Manual (for Husbands/Wives)
Meditations on Proverbs for Couples
Pillow Talk
Questions Couples Ask
Relationships (and workbook)
Saving Your Marriage Before It Starts (and workbooks)
Saving Your Second Marriage Before It Starts (and workbooks)

Video Curriculum — ZondervanGroupware®

Complete Resource Kit for Marriage Mentoring
I Love You More
Love Talk
Mentoring Engaged and Newlywed Couples
Relationships
Saving Your Marriage Before It Starts

Audio

Love Talk
Relationships
Saving Your Marriage Before It Starts
Saving Your Second Marriage Before It Starts

Books by Les Parrott

The Control Freak
Helping Your Struggling Teenager
High Maintenance Relationships
The Life You Want Your Kids to Live
Seven Secrets of a Healthy Dating Relationship
Shoulda, Coulda, Woulda
Once Upon a Family
25 Ways to Win with People (coauthored with John Maxwell)
Love the Life You Live (coauthored with Neil Clark Warren)

Books by Leslie Parrott

If You Ever Needed Friends, It's Now
You Matter More Than You Think
God Loves You Nose to Toes (children's book)
Marshmallow Clouds (children's book)

THE
PARENT
YOU WANT TO BE

Who You Are Matters More Than What You Do

Drs. Les & Leslie Parrott

ZONDERVAN.com/
AUTHORTRACKER
follow your favorite authors

We want to hear from you. Please send your comments about this book to us in care of zreview@zondervan.com. Thank you.

The Parent You Want to Be
Copyright © 2007 by The Foundation for Healthy Relationships

Requests for information should be addressed to:
Zondervan, *Grand Rapids, Michigan 49530*

Library of Congress Cataloging-in-Publication Data

Parrott, Les.
    The parent you want to be : who you are matters more than what you do /
Drs. Les and Leslie Parrott.
       p. cm.
    Includes bibliographical references.
    ISBN-10: 0-310-27245-9 (hardcover)
    ISBN-13: 978-0-310-27245-8 (hardcover)
    1. Parents — Religious life. 2. Self-actualization (Psychology) — Religious aspects —
Christianity. I. Parrott, Leslie L., 1964– II. Title.
BV4529.P385   2007
248.8'45 — dc22
                                          2007006711

This edition printed on acid-free paper.

Published in association with Yates & Yates, LLP, Attorneys and Counselors, Orange, California, and Result Source, Inc., San Diego, California.

Interior design by Beth Shagene

Printed in the United States of America

07 08 09 10 11 12 13 • 24 23 22 21 20 19 18 17 16 15 14 13 12 11 10 9 8 7 6 5 4 3 2 1

To John Leslie Parrott and Jackson Leslie Parrott
The joy you bring us knows no bounds.
Neither does our love for you.

"Don't ever forget."

Contents

PART THREE
BECOMING THE PARENT YOU WANT TO BE

Acknowledgments

The seeds of this book were planted in our hearts shortly after the birth of our first son, but the catalyst for writing it came from a group of friends sitting around a large table in Chicago. We are deeply indebted to Michael Ranville, Barbara Scott, Bob Young, Andy Meisenheimer, and Sandy Vander Zicht.

For the better part of a day, we talked with this group about the ideas you'll soon discover in this book. But it wasn't a one-sided conversation. The room was animated as each of us shared personal thoughts about the kind of parents we want to be. This group helped us hone our thinking and encouraged us more than any writers have the right to be encouraged. Chances are, the book you are holding would probably be sitting dormant in our hearts had these kind friends not encouraged its writing.

We are also grateful to the following people who add to our publishing team: Scott Bolinder, Bruce Ryskamp, Stan Gundry, Joyce Ondersma, Jackie Aldridge, Mark Hunt, John Raymond, T. J. Rathbun, Jeff Bowden, Becky Shingledecker, Sealy Yates, Kevin Small, Karen Campbell, Janice Lundquist, Bill Dallas, and Terry Rouch.

In addition, many parents have either reviewed portions of this manuscript or talked to us at length about the parents they want to be. Each of them has contributed to our thinking along the way. Some of these parents include Kevin and Kathy Lunn, Jeff and Stacy

Kemp, Steve and Thanne Moore, Cliff and Joyce Penner, Mark and Candi Brown, Kevin and Sandi Leman, Scott and Debbie Daniels, Dave and Jan Stoop, Randall and Bonnie Davey, John and Cindy Trent, Jerry and Sharyn Regier, Rodney and Elizabeth Cox, Ken and Stacey Coleman, Doug and Margo Engberg, Dave and Claudia Arp, Steve and Jewell Harmon, Norm and Joyce Wright, Loran and Brenda Lichty, Gary and Carrie Oliver, Jim and Karen Gwinn, Kristin and Jeremy Stendera, Bonnie and Arnie Brann, Tami and Jeff Englehorn, Lori and Brent Hagen, Sandy and Harry Hanson, Arlys and George Osborne, and Joy and Jim Zorn.

We are indebted to the thousands of parents we have met across North America at our marriage seminars. So many of you have asked us, "When are you going to write a parenting book?" We're so glad you asked. Your question spurred on the development of this book as well.

Finally, we want to acknowledge you, our reader. We don't do so glibly. We genuinely appreciate your taking the time to read this book, and we want you to know we've had you in mind at every sentence. Nothing is more gratifying to us, as authors, than to know that the words we've labored over are being read by the people we wrote them for. So thank you, sincerely.

*If you are a parent, recognize that it is the most important
calling and rewarding challenge you have.
What you do every day, what you say and how you act,
will do more to shape America than any other factor.*
Marian Wright Edelman

Getting the Most
from This Book

If we were to sit down at your kitchen table together and ask you what kind of parent you want to be, what would you say? You don't have to answer immediately. Just think about it.

You're probably reading this book in between work, errands, chores, and a myriad of other activities. Or maybe you've taken it with you on a trip where you hope to have some extended time. Wherever you are, we want to thank you for making a connection with us. As the parents of two little boys, we know the challenge of trying to find a few minutes to read a book like this. And we are going to do everything we can to make it worth your effort.

That's why we've posed this question right at the beginning. It's one of the most important questions you will ever explore. Why? Because how you answer it will shape your child's life forever (we'd add an ominous echo effect on that last word if we could).

Too strong? Are we overstating it? We don't think so. After all, if your own parents—no matter how blessed you already may have been to have them raise you—had been more patient, or more affirming, or more visionary, or more (fill in the blank), wouldn't you be a different person than you are today?

Of course. You get the point. So we'll ask again: Knowing that it is impossible to embody every good quality that you might aspire to have as a parent, what are the top traits you'd most like to have?

How you answer this question at the moment, by the way, may change significantly by the time you're done reading this book. So beware. We plan to open your eyes to some qualities to which you may never have given serious attention.

Before you jump into the heart of this book, we want you to know that we've written it with busy parents in mind. You'll soon see that the chapters are brief and that each one is divided by headings that will allow you to set the book aside to change a diaper or take your child to a soccer practice and then easily find your place again to pick up where you left off.

We've also included a few exercises and brief self-tests to help you internalize the material. And we've included discussion questions at the end of each chapter that can be especially helpful in generating positive discussions not only with your spouse but with a small group or even a class of other parents who are invested in being the parents they want to be. After all, a book is never really understood or applied until it is talked about with other people.

Again, thanks for joining us on this journey. We wish you every success in becoming the parent you want to be.

Les and Leslie Parrott
Seattle, Washington

PART ONE

YOUR KIDS WILL REMEMBER YOUR TRAITS

CHAPTER 1

How Does Your Child Perceive You?

*Before I got married,
I had six theories about bringing up children.
Now I have six children and no theories.*
John Wilmot

"Dad," my first grader asked me recently, "what are you going to do when you come to my class for Parents' Day?" He was standing on the opposite side of my desk in my home study.

"What have the other parents done?" I asked, looking up from my computer screen, where I'd been replying to email messages.

"Anthony's dad let each of us try on his fireman's helmet and heavy jacket," he said excitedly. "It was heavy, and it smelled like smoke! And you know what, Dad?"

"What, John?"

"Anthony's dad rescues people from burning buildings with a big ax! Have you ever done that, Dad?"

"Well, no. I haven't done that," I replied, clearing my throat. "What have other parents done when they've come to your class?"

"Audrey's dad works at the Museum of Flight, and he set off a really big rocket for us on the playground—it was so cool! You should have seen the smoke!"

"Mm-hmm."

"It went so high, Dad. It had sparks and everything!"

"That sounds really cool," I slowly murmured.

"Nick's mom is a doctor," John continued, "and she put a cast on Nick's arm right there in the class, and then she cut off the cast and passed it around the room so we could touch it—but Tayden didn't want to because he said it was gross."

> It is no use walking anywhere to preach unless our walking is our preaching.
>
> **St. Francis of Assisi**

"Wow!" I said, trying to join in on his excitement.

"So what are you going to do, Dad?" John asked earnestly.

"Well, Son, let's see. Um, what do you think I should do?"

"Mommy says you work at your computer and talk on the phone a lot."

"Is that what Mommy says? I guess she's right about that—but I don't think I want to do that for your class."

"Nooo!" John giggled.

"Let me talk to your mom about Parents' Day."

With that, John scampered out to the backyard as I tracked down Leslie in the kitchen. "What am I supposed to do in John's class for Parents' Day? John's going to think I'm the most boring dad in the world, and he'll remember this forever," I said frantically.

Leslie started laughing.

"I'm serious."

"I know. I just got a mental image of you showing the class how you talk on your cell phone and write at your computer."

"Very funny!" I snapped. "John already told me that joke—and I didn't laugh then either."

Just then John came in from the backyard and said, "Hey, Dad, why don't you bring your brain to class?"

He wasn't joking. John had once sat in on one of my lectures at the university where I talked about the human brain. I'd used an actual human brain from a formaldehyde container I borrowed from the biology department. Needless to say, he was fascinated—as were my college students.

And that's exactly what I did for Parents' Day. I explained to his first grade class that I'm a "doctor" who works on feelings and that feelings begin in the brain. I showed them a colorful wooden model of the brain and then asked if they'd like to see an actual brain that I had in a jar contained in a cardboard box.

"Yes—show us the brain!" some students shouted.

"Children, let's be respectful now," John's teacher said with authority while keeping an eye on the cardboard box.

The kids were now literally sitting on the edge of their seats, and John was grinning from ear to ear. The anticipation in that first grade classroom was palpable. I put on my protective goggles and latex gloves before reaching into the box. The children were wide-eyed— except for Tayden. He was peeking through his fingers.

I spent the next few minutes answering one question after another. The questions ranged from the practical ("What are all those lines on it?") to the curious ("Whose brain is it?") to the theological ("Doesn't he need his brain in heaven?").

Needless to say, I was a hit. The kids still talk about that day when they see me picking up John after school. And so does John. "Remember when you brought the brain to my school, Dad?" he'll say. "That was awesome!"

Whew! I did it. I made my son proud. And isn't that what every parent wants? Don't you want your child's perception of you to be as positive as possible?

Your Child Aspires to Be Like You — Is That a Good Thing?

That afternoon after buckling John into his car seat and traveling back home from school, Leslie and I were talking about what we might do for dinner. Then, during a brief lull, John said something that would melt any parent's heart: "Dad, I want to be like you."

The truth is, whether our kids say it or not, they feel it. Children aspire to become what their parents are. And that's precisely why it's critical to be the kind of parents we want to be.

John's comment got me to thinking. If he wanted to be like me, how did he perceive me? What qualities did he see in me that he wanted to emulate? Suddenly I was more self-conscious than I'd been in years. I felt like I was sixteen again, looking into the mirror and wondering what other people thought of me. Metaphorically, I began to "check myself out." Was I a patient man? Could my son look at me and say, "I want to be patient like Dad is"? Was I optimistic? I sure wanted my son to be. Was I forgiving, empathic, comforting, kind?

> I talk and talk and talk, and I haven't taught people in fifty years what my father taught me by example in one week.
>
> **Mario Cuomo**

Have you ever had these same thoughts? What traits does your child see in you? Perhaps more important, what traits doesn't your child see in you that you wish he or she did?

From the day John was born, I was so focused on what I would *do* as a parent — reading all kinds of books on techniques and strategies — that I hadn't given much thought to the kind of parent I wanted to *be*.

Leslie felt the same way. And the more we talked about it, the more serious we became about what we've come to call "intentional traits." Each of us made a list of the top five traits we wanted to be sure our children saw in us. And our lists were very different. What's more, some of the traits came naturally and easily to one or the other of us, while other traits would require more work.

Who You Are Matters More Than What You Do

Now don't misunderstand—we're all for using good parenting techniques to discipline and motivate our children. In fact, you'll find many practical parenting tips in this book. But the primary message we want to get across is this: Your child's character hinges on the traits you exhibit as a parent. And who you are as a parent isn't left to fate, luck, or chance. You can *choose* to be the kind of parent you want to be. While plenty of things about your child's life are unpredictable and beyond your control, you can make certain your child has a parent with particular qualities. This book will show you how.

You may be wondering why the traits you embody even matter. Let's make this plain: Your traits matter because your child is watching you more closely than you know. A haunting reminder of just how powerful we are as parental role models is found in the Harry Chapin classic "Cat's in the Cradle." Written in 1974, this song starts out with a natural harmony and depicts the tale of a father with his newborn son. The first time we hear the chorus, the dad is saying:

> *And he was talking 'fore I knew it, and as he grew,*
> *He'd say, "I'm gonna be like you, Dad.*
> *You know I'm gonna be like you."*

But by the end of the tune, which has followed their relationship through the boy's tenth birthday, his college years, and finally the father's retirement, the chorus is bittersweet. It seems the son, who has moved away and started his own family, picked up on the one quality his father hoped he wouldn't pass along—the quality of being too busy for relationships. The father has called his son to see if the two of them can get together. "I'd love to, Dad, if I could find the time," answers his son. In the final chorus, the father's words ring true:

And as I hung up the phone, it occurred to me,
He'd grown up just like me.
My boy was just like me.

Chapin's song will stop almost every parent dead in their tracks. And if it doesn't, it should. It's a poignant reminder to take stock of the traits, both good and bad, that our children observe in us.

Being a parent — not just *doing* parental things — is the most important calling you will ever have. But it's also the most rewarding enterprise of your life — especially when you are the parent you want to be.

For Discussion

1. How would your child describe you to another person? What specific traits would your child mention?

2. If your child grows up to be just like you in one way, what way do you hope that is and why?

3. Do you agree that when it comes to parenting, who you are matters more than what you do? Why or why not?

CHAPTER 2

Identifying Your Personal Parenting Traits

What we are teaches the child far more than what we say,
so we must be what we want our children to become.
Joseph Chilton Pearce

Salish Lodge is a romantic mountain retreat just thirty miles from our home in Seattle. Overlooking the breathtaking Snoqualmie Falls, you can hear the roar of white water tumbling over granite cliffs nearly three hundred feet into the emerald river canyon below. Rain or shine, you can venture down the pine tree–lined trail by day and let the crackling of your own wood-burning fireplace soothe you to sleep by night.

Ranked as one of the finest lodging, dining, and spa facilities in the world, the lodge has provided the backdrop for some very special moments in our lives. But one of our most meaningful Salish Lodge getaways came five years ago when we hired a babysitter to watch our three-year-old while we dedicated twenty-four hours of uninterrupted time to thinking about parenting. More specifically, we were thinking about the two of us as parents.

It started with a leisurely lunch the first day and ended with a laid-back brunch on the second. In between we enjoyed a scrumptious five-course dinner. At each of those meals, the topic of conversation was the same: What kind of parents do we want to be—and what kinds of kids do we want to raise?

We weren't talking about parenting techniques, philosophies, or strategies. We weren't discussing a parenting book or a class we had taken. We were exploring what we have come to call our "personal parenting traits." In other words, we were taking a hard look at our unique personalities and even the personalities of our own parents who raised us. Why? Because a wise mentor in our graduate school days, as we were training to be psychologists, said something that stuck. "More important than what you *do* as a parent," he said, "is who you *are* as a parent." He went on to explain that you can buy into any number of parenting strategies, but each and every one of them will be overshadowed by the personal qualities you bring to parenting.

> Good food ends with good talk.
>
> **Geoffrey Neighor**

Getting Real about Who We Are as Parents

We learned a lot about each other over our leisurely meals at Salish Lodge, especially about each other's childhoods. We talked about what we admired and appreciated in our own parents. Les, for example, told me that some of the best things his parents ever did for him involved celebrating his successes and helping him dream about his future and plan for a meaningful life. And I shared with Les that I deeply appreciated how prayerful my parents were and how safe they made me feel through their dedication to me.

We also talked about what we wished our parents had done for us that they hadn't. After all, while both of us were blessed to be raised in loving homes, we are well aware that no parents are perfect. I talked to Les about the fact that my family rarely cared about external accomplishments. My mom and dad barely reviewed my report card. I can't remember a time they acknowledged a good grade or worried about a poor one. And Les confessed that his parents were often unpredictable, changing or canceling events he'd looked forward to.

During one conversation, we talked about what we saw in each other that would make each of us a good parent. For example, knowing Les's sense of humor, I said he would be a fun parent who would fill our children's lives with lots of laughter. And he pointed out that I would find numerous occasions, not just birthdays, to celebrate our children's milestones to make them feel special.

But then came the tough part. Over brunch we dedicated our conversation to discovering what each of us would need to be better at if we were going to be the best parents we could be. You got it—we lowered our defenses, straightened our backs, and got real about our unique personalities and how they could potentially diminish our effectiveness as parents.

Les was the first to open up. "I think my number one hurdle on the road to being the parent I want to be is going to be my hard-driving work style." I couldn't have said it better myself, but I didn't even nod. I just listened. "I don't want to be a father who is preoccupied and distracted. I want to be connected and attentive—really tuned in to my child's life." When Les finished, he genuinely invited my feedback. We talked for a good half hour about how his hardwired drive to produce and accomplish could interfere with his parenting—*and* how it could be rechanneled as an attribute that would help him be the kind of father he wanted to be.

> Love must be fed and nurtured. . . . First and foremost it demands time.
>
> **David Mace**

When my turn came to share, I knew what had to be said. "I am such a pleaser, I know I'm going to have to work extra hard to be authentic as a parent." Les returned the favor of just listening as I talked. "I know my personality will drive me to do things for my children I shouldn't do. I know it will crush me to see them suffer and I'll want to intervene when I shouldn't." I went on to talk about the precautions I'd have to take to avoid being a pushover parent.

Getting Real about the Kind of Kids We Want to Raise

We didn't devote all of our conversations on this getaway to our traits as parents. In fact, over lunch on that first day, we got things rolling by talking about the traits we wanted our children to have.

"What kind of a man do you want John to be in twenty years?" I asked Les.

He didn't answer right away. Instead, he sat pensively, fiddling with his fork on the linen tablecloth while looking out the plate glass window to the Snoqualmie River Canyon below. "I want my son to be deeply secure in who he is — like those huge rocks down there," he finally said. "I don't want him to be a man without backbone, swayed by the current of any old thing that somebody wants him to do or think. I hope he's strong and confident."

"Wow," I said, "you've given this some thought."

"Not really," Les confessed. "I just know I want to raise a kid who doesn't cave in to peer pressure. What about you?"

"I want John to be the kind of man who is genuinely kind, you know? I hope we raise him to be sensitive to other people and really caring."

> If I could make only one wish for a child, I'd wish him the quality of lovingness.
>
> **Benjamin Spock**

Les grinned widely, then began to chuckle.

"What's so funny?"

"Nothing — it's just that our answers are so male/female, so gender oriented, don't you think? I mean, I want him to be secure and strong like one of those boulders down there, and you want him to be tender and sensitive."

We both laughed about our stereotypical answers. But we kept talking. In fact, we talked for at least another hour about the traits we wanted our son to have as a result of growing up in our home. We discussed the fact that his own God-given personality would dictate much of who he will be—regardless of what we bring to his life. But we kept talking about who we might help him to become within that context. Eventually we came up with a list of traits describing the kind of person we hoped John, and any eventual siblings he might have, would grow up to be.

Here are some of the characteristics we wrote on a note card that afternoon:

- Emotionally secure in his personhood
- Hopeful about his personal future
- Relationally savvy and connected to others
- Persistent in his goals and undertakings
- Respectful and kind toward friends and strangers
- Thoughtful and effective in his decision making
- Deeply reverent toward God and grounded in his Word

These traits weren't in any particular order, and our list wasn't exhaustive. But it was enough to guide us toward the qualities we would need to embody if we wanted to raise this kind of child.

Making Our Own List of Personal Parenting Traits

By the time our personal parenting retreat came to an end, we had a good grasp on what we needed to do. Strike that. We had a good grasp on *who* we needed to become. In fact, the traits we noted during that retreat have shaped the traits that make up the basic outline of this book. But there's more to parenting than our own influence.

Once we had formed a rough list of the personal traits we wanted to embody as parents—some of them, by the way, being more important to one or the other of us—we eventually shared it with an intimate group of friends who met us for this very purpose in Chicago.

We hadn't shared our list with anyone since we had made it at Salish Lodge nearly five years earlier. But after seeing how our own list had so positively impacted our personal parenting, we knew we wanted to share this exercise with other parents.

> Having children makes you no more a parent than having a piano makes you a pianist.
>
> **Michael Levine**

So, after connecting over a superb Italian dinner, we met our friends around a large conference table at a Chicago hotel and began talking about parenting. We put up three or four easels around the room with plenty of paper to write on. Some of our friends had newborns; others were seasoned parents.

"Okay," Les started, "most of you are parents, and some of you hope to be parents someday. What we want to know is what kind of parents you want to be. When you think about the traits that you want your son or daughter to observe in you, what comes to mind?"

With that, we were off and running. Les was filling up the easel pages with one trait after another. The group members were energized by the exercise, wanting to expound on each trait they mentioned and why it was important to them as parents.

Our next step was to take the two dozen or so traits we'd listed and begin surveying other groups of parents to see which of these traits had the broadest relevance. Our goal was to whittle down the list to a manageable size by consolidating traits that overlapped and eliminating traits that appealed to only a small fraction of parents. And that's just what we did.

Ten Traits Worth Considering

After surveying hundreds of parents about the personal parenting traits they desire to exemplify, we have identified ten traits that seem to matter most. In other words, we've identified the ten traits that received the most votes.

Here's some background on the survey: Almost all of the respondents were churchgoing couples who either were expecting a baby or already had children. They ranged in age from midtwenties to early forties. And when presented with a list of more than twenty parental traits, they ranked the following ten traits the highest:

- Affirming
- Patient
- Attentive
- Visionary
- Connecting
- Celebratory
- Authentic
- Comforting
- Insightful
- Prayerful

Because the degree of difference between the ranks of these traits was so minimal in our survey, we have not listed them in any particular order. We've simply plucked out the top ten as a place to help parents like you begin thinking about your own parenting traits.

In the next chapter, we give you an opportunity to make this list of traits more personal.

For Discussion

1. Before you picked up this book, when was the last time you had a meaningful conversation about being the parent you want to be? What did you learn as a result?

2. If you could press a magic button that would automatically ensure that your child would have three qualities you desire, what would those qualities be and why?

3. As you read about the "ten traits worth considering," which ones were you most surprised to see listed and why?

CHAPTER 3

How to Become
the Parent You Want to Be:
An Exercise

Parenting will eventually produce bizarre behavior,
and I'm not talking about the kids.
Their behavior is always normal.
Bill Cosby

A young father in a supermarket was pushing a shopping cart with his young son, who was strapped in the front. The little boy was irritable, fussing and crying. The other shoppers gave the pair a wide berth because the child would pull products off shelves and throw them on the floor. The father seemed to be very calm; as he continued down each aisle, he murmured gently, "Easy now, Donald. Keep calm, Donald. Steady, boy. It's all right, Donald."

A mother who was passing by was greatly impressed by this young father's solicitous attitude. She said, "You certainly know how to talk to an upset child — quietly and gently."

And then bending down to the little boy, she asked, "What seems to be the trouble, Donald?"

"Oh no," said the father. "He's Henry. I'm Donald."

Though we don't recommend ignoring a child's wrong behavior, Donald knows the

> My father didn't tell me how to live; he lived, and let me watch him do it.
> **Clarence Budington Kelland**

struggle of trying to be the parent he wants to be. And like most other parents on the planet, he is working hard to do just that. The intent of this book is to make this work a whole lot easier.

Identifying Your Personal Parenting Profile

In chapter 2 we described our personal parenting retreat at Salish Lodge outside of Seattle, but you don't need to schedule a retreat to come up with a plan for becoming the parent you want to be. In fact, you can do it in a matter of minutes with what we are about to show you.

What follows is a simple discussion guide to help you give serious thought to the kind of parent you aspire to be. We've designed this exercise so you can work through it with your spouse, but you can do much of it on your own if you prefer.

> We are apt to forget that children watch examples better than they listen to preaching.
> **Roy L. Smith**

By the way, if you visit our website, www. RealRelationships.com, you can download a complimentary discussion guide (one for husbands, one for wives) to make this exercise that much easier. And if you are using this book in a small group or class, the discussion guide can be quite useful in facilitating your discussions. But if you don't have access to a computer, don't worry—you can still do the exercise right from this book. You don't even need a pen.

The exercise includes four sections and can take anywhere from a few minutes to a couple of hours, depending on how deeply you'd like to explore each area. You can make a date of it over coffee or do one section at a time, if need be, so you won't be interrupted by the kids, pagers, or cell phones. And if you are absolutely rushed for time and eager to dive into the other chapters of this book, you can jump to section 4. The choice is yours.

Let's Get Started*

Section 1: Exploring Where You Came From

This first section is designed to help each of you better understand the people who have shaped you most in your role as parents. If you and your spouse are completing this section of the exercise together, take turns answering the following questions.

1. Describe some of your most vivid positive memories as a child with your parents. What stands out and why?
2. What admirable qualities did your father have that shaped the person you've become? Give some specific examples of how these qualities made you a better person. What did he do that made these qualities evident? What can you do to emulate them?
3. What admirable qualities did your mother have that shaped the person you've become? Give some specific examples of how these qualities made you a better person. What did she do that made these qualities evident? What can you do to emulate them?
4. What qualities do you think were missing in either one of your parents? How would you be a better person if your parents had exemplified these traits?

Section 2: Sharing Your Self-Reflection

This second section facilitates a bit of inner exploration of your personality and shows you how your personality can't help but shape you as a parent — for good and for not so good.

------

* If you are a single parent, we have a special message for you in an appendix at the back of this book; it contains information regarding how you can benefit from this exercise in relation to your personal situation. We recommend you read it before coming back to this chapter.

1. Because of your natural hard-wiring, what one or two positive traits do you instinctively bring to the enterprise of parenting? How do these positive traits shape your child?
2. Take a deep breath, do some honest reflection, and identify one or two traits you currently lack that would significantly improve your effectiveness as a parent. In other words, what missing trait is likely to be your biggest hurdle on the road to becoming the parent you want to be?

Section 3: Inviting

This third section gets more personal, so do your best to put your guard down and cultivate a receptive heart and listening ears. The goal is to learn a bit more about yourself—like when you look in the mirror.

1. Invite your spouse to share with you one trait that he or she sees in you that makes you a great parent.
2. Invite your spouse to share with you one trait that he or she perceives to be deficient in you—a trait that would make you a more effective parent. This is a time to invite feedback and avoid defensiveness.

The day the child realizes that all adults are imperfect, he becomes an adolescent; the day he forgives them, he becomes an adult; the day he forgives himself, he becomes wise.

Alden Nowlan

Section 4: Identifying Your Top Two Traits

Finally, we want you to review the list of the "ten traits worth considering" (see below). These are the same ten traits we introduced in chapter 2 — the same ten that make up the coming chapters in this book. Your job is to do two things:

1. First, identify two traits from the list that you believe you are most naturally inclined to embody. In other words, which two traits come easiest to you? While you're at it, identify the two traits that you think come easiest to your spouse (this can make for good discussion).

2. Second, identify two traits that you believe would make you a better parent. In other words, which two traits do you currently lack but seek to attain? And if you have more than one child, do you wish to exemplify more of a certain trait with each unique child?

Here, with more amplification, are the "ten traits worth considering":

Comes Easily *Needs Work*

□	□	Giving the Praise They Crave: Being an *Affirming* Parent
□	□	Counting to Ten — Again: Being a *Patient* Parent
□	□	Hearing What They Don't Say: Being an *Attentive* Parent
□	□	Seeing a Picture of Their Future: Being a *Visionary* Parent
□	□	Building a Better Bond: Being a *Connected* Parent
□	□	Commemorating Milestones: Being a *Celebratory* Parent
□	□	Keeping Your Word: Being an *Authentic* Parent
□	□	Creating the Safest Place on Earth: Being a *Comforting* Parent
□	□	Instilling Wisdom: Being an *Insightful* Parent
□	□	Practicing the Presence of God: Being a *Prayerful* Parent

Once you've completed the four sections of this exercise, be sure to talk them over with your spouse, taking as much or as little time as you like.

> Children will invariably talk, eat, walk, think, respond, and act like their parents. Give them a target to shoot at. Give them a goal to work toward. Give them a pattern that they can see clearly, and you give them something that gold and silver cannot buy.
>
> **Billy Graham**

Before You Move On

In a famous sociological case study looking at changes in the small Midwest city of Muncie, Indiana, in 1924, mothers were asked to rank the qualities they most desired in their children. At the top of the list were conformity and strict obedience. More than fifty years later, when the Middletown survey was replicated, mothers placed autonomy and independence first.[1]

Times change, and so does parenting. In fact, it changes from parent to parent. That's why we don't want you to think of the ten traits in this book as exhaustive. When you completed the exercise earlier in this chapter, you may have identified a very important trait that is missing from the list or perhaps subsumed in another. It may have been a trait your own parents displayed. That's okay. The intent of this list is simply to get you thinking and talking about the traits that many parents view as important—and ultimately to help you become the parent you want to be.

As you move into the next section of this book, feel free to read the coming chapters in any order you like. Each is freestanding and not predicated on any of the others, so if you want to skip ahead to the two chapters that interest you most, feel free.

As you read through the coming chapters, by the way, you may want to come back to section 4 of the exercise in this chapter and revise your answers. Even as we wrote this book, we found ourselves shifting our allegiances to traits that we didn't find very important to us personally until we researched them.

Finally, remember that none of us is a perfect parent. And even being a good parent doesn't guarantee your child will turn out exactly as you wish. You can count on some rocky roads with every child.

So let's make something clear right now: This book doesn't promise to make you a perfect ten in each of the ten traits we're about to explore. If that was our goal, we'd title this book *The Parent We Want You to Be*. Ridiculous! Children are too complex, as are parents, to prescribe one profile to fit everyone. So rest easy. We're not pushing each of these traits on you. We're simply saying that each of them is worthy of your consideration. And some of them—at least the two you selected in the exercise earlier in this chapter—will help you become the parent *you* want to be.

For Discussion

1. The exercise in this chapter has given you plenty to discuss already. However, if you are exploring this information together with other parents in a small group or class, ask each other what insights you gained from the exercise.

2. Again, if you are in a group context, take turns sharing which two of the ten traits you believe you are most naturally inclined to embody and why you think so.

3. Finally, share the two traits you believe would make you a better parent, and if you feel comfortable doing so, invite the group to give you feedback on them.

PART TWO

TEN TRAITS WORTH CONSIDERING

Giving the Praise They Crave: Are You an *Affirming* Parent?

*Parents need to fill a child's bucket
of self-esteem so high
that the rest of the world can't poke
enough holes in it to drain it dry.*
Alvin Price

Storyteller extraordinaire Garrison Keillor, in his book *We Are Still Married*, gives an account of a baseball team named the Lake Wobegon Schroeders, so named because the starting nine were brothers, sons of E. J. Schroeder. And everybody in the small town of Lake Wobegon knew that E. J. never affirmed his boys. If one of them hit a bad pitch, says Keillor, he'd spit and curse and rail at him. And if a son hit a home run, E. J. would say, "Blind man coulda hit that one. Your gramma coulda put the wood on that one. If a guy couldn't hit that one out, there'd be something wrong with him, I'd say. Wind practically took that one out of here, didn't even need to hit it much"—and then he'd lean over and spit.

On one occasion, his eldest son, Edwin Jim Jr., turned and ran to the center field fence for a long, long, long fly ball. He threw his glove forty feet in the air to snag the ball. Amazingly, he caught the ball and glove to win the game. When the boy turned toward the dugout to see if his dad had seen the catch, E. J. was on his feet clapping, but when he saw his son look to him, he immediately pretended he was swatting mosquitoes. When Jim ran back to the bench and stood by his dad,

43

> The meanest, most contemptible kind of praise is that which first speaks well of a man, and then qualifies it with a "but."
>
> **Henry Ward Beecher**

E. J. sat chewing in silence and finally said, "I saw a man in Superior, Wisconsin, do that a long time ago. But he did it at night, and the ball was hit a lot harder."[1]

Now, chances are, you wouldn't even imagine withholding affirmation from your child the way E. J. did. At least, we hope not! But if you're honest, affirmation may be one of the traits you need to dust off and practice more often. Why? Because far too many parents are afraid of overdoing it with praise—and that's nearly impossible. We'll underscore the value of appropriate affirmation in a moment, but first let's be sure we know exactly what the word *affirming* means.

AFFIRMING AFFIRMING AFFIRMING AFFIRMING AFFIRMING AFFIRMING AFFIRMING AFFIRMING

You already know that an affirmation is a positive statement, as in "You did a great job, and I'm proud of you." Affirmation occurs whenever you make your child feel noticed, valued, and special.

But the word *affirm* actually goes deeper than that. If you study its origin, you'll find its roots are in the Latin *affirmare*, from *ad* + *firmare*, meaning "to make firm." So when you affirm a child, you are, in a very real sense, equipping him with a firm foundation of self-respect and self-esteem. Affirmations, in other words, provide a solid platform to stand on. They give a child emotional security. Without them, a child is far more likely to feel shaky, anxious, and insecure.

The Undeniable Importance of Being an Affirming Parent

Dan Baber honored his mother by posting an auction on eBay titled "Best Mother in the World." The winning bidder would receive an email from his mom, Sue Hamilton, that Baber promised would "make you feel like you are the most special person on the Earth."

How did people respond to Baber's offer? During the auction's seven-day run, 42,711 people—enough to fill most baseball stadiums—took a look. Ninety-two people bid, pushing the price from a $1 opening bid to a $610 closing bid!

Isn't it interesting that so many adults are willing to pay for a mother's affirmation? This says something about how valuable it is. Sadly, it also reveals how many children don't get enough of it as they're growing up. In fact, the *Chicago Tribune* reports that only 20 percent of parents actually do a good job affirming their children.[2]

One reason for parents' less-than-stellar affirmation of their kids is that they don't recognize the profound worth of affirmation in a child's life. They think lavishing their kids with praise might give them "big heads." They've bought into the lousy advice of Samuel Johnson, who said, "Praise, like gold and diamonds, owes its value only to its scarcity." No, no, no. Praise, when given from a sincere parent, is most valuable in abundance. The risk of building up an oversized ego is negligible.

Think of it this way. Your child has a hole in her heart that can be filled only by her parents' praise. And if she doesn't receive enough affirmation from you, she'll go her whole life trying desperately to find it. She'll try her best, even as a grown woman, to do anything she can to please you and win your affirmation—and eventually the affirmation of everyone else.

> If a child lives with approval, he learns to live with himself.
>
> **Dorothy Law Nolte**

In fact, nearly every psychologist would agree with us when we say that nothing ensures the likelihood of an insecure adult more than a child who doesn't receive enough affirmation growing up. We've seen it countless times in our counseling office. A grown adult, suffering from a childhood affirmation deficiency, comes in because he has a hole in his heart that has become so emotionally taxing that he is now desperate to repair the poor choices (from workaholism to materialism to unhealthy relationships to addictions) he has made to fill it.

A Self-Test: How Affirming Are You?

The following true/false self-test is designed to get your wheels turning. Don't worry about trying to get the "right" answer; just give the answer that lines up with what you currently believe.

- T   F   My child knows I value and appreciate him whether I say it or not.
- T   F   It's more important to affirm a child's character than her performance.
- T   F   The best affirmations exaggerate the importance of a child's work.
- T   F   When a child's personality is praised directly ("You're a smart boy"), he will come to believe what I say.
- T   F   You should affirm a child only when she has done something worthy of affirmation.

Scoring: If you answered "true" to any of these five items, you will benefit from brushing up on how to affirm your child. Even if you answered "false" to each of these items, you can always learn new ways to become more affirming.

How to Become an Affirming Parent

It's difficult to exaggerate how deeply a child needs to be affirmed by his parents. Consider the award-winning actor Jamie Foxx. He never had the relationship with his father that he wanted. His biological parents lived twenty-eight miles away in Dallas, Texas, but rarely visited or noted his achievements. "I passed for more than one thousand yards, the first quarterback at my high school to do that," says Foxx. "I was making the *Dallas Morning News*, and my father never came down. Even to this day nothing but that absence makes me angry."[3]

> To praise is an investment in happiness.
> **George M. Adams**

Understandably so. Sometimes all it takes to affirm a child's efforts is your presence. Of course, we can do a whole lot better than that. Let's look at some of the most proven practices of affirming parents.

Affirming Parents Praise What Their Children Do — Not Who They Are

Recently our first grader brought home a second-place ribbon for running the one-hundred-yard dash at his first grade field day. He had a mile-wide smile as he held up his prize. Our first impulse was to say something like, "John, you are such a fast runner!" But we didn't. Instead, we showered him with praise for his efforts and accomplishment. Here's how the conversation unfolded:

Leslie: What a race!
John: I know. I ran really fast!
Les: You sure did. You ran so hard. I could tell you were really giving it your all.
John: I'm a fast runner, Daddy.

Did you notice in this short exchange that it was John who was making inferences about himself? In other words, we didn't tell our son, "You're a fast runner"; John came to this conclusion on his own. And that's the point. A parent's praise should be phrased in such a way that the child draws positive inferences about himself—rather than being labeled positively by the parent.

Why does this matter? Because praise and affirmation, when applied to a child's personality (and an adult's, too, for that matter), can create undue pressure that has negative results.

Let's take another example. Say Jennifer, age nine, does a good job cleaning up her room. She puts away her clothes, makes her bed, straightens up her toys, and so on. Her mother is impressed and says, "You are such a wonderful child."

Jennifer smiles in appreciation.

"You are truly Mother's little helper."

What's wrong with this scenario? Nothing, on the face of it. But such positive comments about who Jennifer is can cause anxiety. She may feel she is far from being wonderful and will never be able to live up to her mom's label. Instead of fearfully waiting to be exposed as a fraud, she may decide to lessen her burden by quickly making a mess or by confessing a misbehavior that proves she really isn't "wonderful."

> Good words are worth much, and cost little.
>
> **George Herbert**

Moreover, a child whose personality is praised directly may not only reject the praise but also have second thoughts about the parent who has praised her: "If Mom finds me so great, she can't be very smart."

Affirming Parents Make Their Affirmations Realistic

When our son John shares a toy or a piece of candy with his younger brother, Jackson, we're likely to say, "That is such a kind thing to do, John. That really makes my heart feel good." What we try to stay away from are phrases such as "You are an angel," or "You are always so considerate." Why? Because it isn't true. John isn't always considerate—and he knows it.

As renowned child psychologist Haim Ginott, author of *Between Parent and Child*, noted, "Direct praise of personality, like direct sunlight, is uncomfortable and blinding. It is embarrassing for a person to be told that he is wonderful, angelic, generous and humble. He feels called upon to deny at least part of the praise."[4]

> Praise your children openly, reprehend them secretly.
> **W. Cecil**

The point is, our words of affirmation should state clearly and realistically what we appreciate about a child's effort, help, or achievement. They should be framed in such a way that the child can draw his own realistic conclusions about his personality. If, based on positive comments about his behavior, he concludes that he is generous, for example, his generosity will be genuine. He will paint a positive picture of himself and won't feel that his generosity is for show or to win approval. And he won't be driven to show you how unrealistic your appraisal of his personality actually is. When a child draws positive conclusions from a parent's realistic affirmations, he is building a healthy personality.

Affirming Parents Know a Child Need Not Perform to Be Affirmed

In our earlier definition of *affirmation*, we pointed out that it occurs whenever you make your child feel noticed, valued, and special. Consequently, your child doesn't have to do much of anything to receive affirmation from you. She doesn't have to win a race or clean her room. She just has to be. That's the true gift of an affirming parent—the recognition of your child's intrinsic value. This kind of affirmation is different from the positive acknowledgment of your child's actions. But notice that it doesn't conflict with our earlier advice to "praise what your children do—not who they are." It comes straight from your heart, regardless of what your child has or hasn't done.

The simple act of telling your child you value him, love him, care for him, and think about him is affirming. In fact, straightforward statements like these are the best affirmations you can give. Why? Because children who have to perform to be affirmed retain a nagging uncertainty about where they stand. They may conclude that they are worthwhile only if they are doing something that draws your attention and wins your approval. And as they grow into adults, this feeling becomes hollow and makes them continually question their self-worth.

> Praise does wonders for our sense of hearing.
>
> **Arnold H. Glasow**

So don't neglect to affirm your child by saying things like, "Do you know I couldn't wait to get home to see you tonight?" "I'm so glad you're my little girl." "My heart smiles every time I think of you." "Being with you is the best part of my day."

Affirming Parents Realize True Affirmations Come from the Heart

Remember that an affirmation is not just something you give; it's something you are. In other words, affirmations are expressed not only through your words but through your being. Your kids pick up affirmations over time as they experience them day upon day and conversation upon conversation.

American writer Eric Hoffer, who was awarded the Presidential Medal of Freedom by Ronald Regan in February 1983, said something interesting about Martha Bauer, the woman who raised him after his mother died. "I remember a lot of talk and a lot of laughter," said Hoffer. "I must have talked a great deal because Martha used to say again and again, 'You remember you said this, you said that....' She remembered everything I said, and all my life I've had the feeling that what I think and what I say are worth remembering. She gave me that."[5]

This kind of affirmation doesn't come from telling your child, "You say such memorable things," or "I love listening to you." Though nothing is wrong with these kinds of statements, how much richer and more meaningful is the affirmation that comes from the heart and is built up over time by your sheer presence.

For Discussion

1. On a scale of 1 to 10, how would you rank the importance of being an affirming parent? Why?

2. On that same scale, how would you rank your natural inclination to give the praise your child craves?

3. Do you agree that parents should praise what their children do rather than who they are? Why or why not?

4. In what specific area of your child's life would you like to be more affirming? When is the next time you will have an opportunity to affirm your child in this area?

CHAPTER 5

Counting to Ten — Again: Are You a *Patient* Parent?

You can learn many things from children.
How much patience you have, for instance.
Franklin P. Jones

Ray Charles was a pioneering pianist and singer who shaped the sound of rhythm and blues. He brought a soulful sound to everything from country music to pop standards to a now-famous rendition of "America the Beautiful." Frank Sinatra called him "the only true genius in the business."

If you've watched the biographical movie of his life, *Ray*, you know all about the trials, challenges, successes, and addictions of the late artist. When we saw it, the most compelling part of the film for both of us showed how Ray compensated for his blindness by learning to hear what others couldn't.

As a blind ten-year-old, Ray enters his home and accidentally trips on the side of a rocking chair. He falls, yells out in pain, and calls to his mother for help. His mother steps forward, stops, hesitates, and takes a step back. Ray, lying on a rug on the floor, continues to cry for his mother's help.

His mother silently goes back to her work. Ray hears men chattering and a hen clucking. He stops crying, tilts his head, and slowly gets up. He hears more people talking, a cow mooing, and metal clanking. He looks in the direction of a kettle of boiling water.

53

Stretching out his arms, he walks toward a crackling fireplace and feels its heat, pulling back a hand when it comes too close. His mother continues to look on, concerned with his every move. Ray listens intently as a horse and carriage go by.

He then hears a chirping grasshopper nearby and walks toward it. He bends down and, fumbling a bit, encloses the grasshopper in his hand. Smiling, he picks it up and puts it to his ear. His mother, taken aback, releases a soft gasp.

> Patience to the soul is as bread to the body.
> **Thomas Adams**

Ray says, "I hear you, Mama. You're right there."

His mother now has tears streaming down her face. She tells him, "Yes, yes, I am." Then she kneels in front of him and gives him a hug.

Whoa! Talk about a patient parent!

Most of the time we think about demonstrating patience as parents when our children are slow to act—slow to tie their shoes, for example. But we can show patience on many levels on any given day.

PATIENT PATIENT PATIENT PATIENT PATIENT PATIENT PATIENT PATIENT PATIENT PATIENT PATIENT PATIE

The term *patient* emphasizes calmness, self-control, and the willingness or ability to tolerate delay. But it involves more. It's a kind of good-natured forbearance. It's uncomplaining endurance.

If you boil patience down to its essence, it is the loving response to frustration. Think about it. Frustration tests our patience threshold. If you have ever watched a small child trying to thread a needle, your patience has been tested. You see the child trying again and again to push the frayed end of the thread through the eye of an unsteady needle. Do you wait two trials, four trials, six trials before snatching it away and doing it yourself? How much frustration can you tolerate before intervening? How long can you suffer? Long enough to take a quiet breath and let her eventually ask for help?

Patience "suffers long" because it resists the impulse to let irritation get the better of us. The word *patience* is related to *patient*—a person who is suffering. The Latin origins of the word reveal that a patient is someone who "bears affliction with calmness." But you don't need to have a medical condition to do that. Every patient parent on the planet suffers long or "bears affliction with calmness" on a routine basis.

The Undeniable Importance of Being a Patient Parent

Not long ago, over boiled eggs and bagels, I (Leslie) was helping my eight-year-old review his spelling words—the ones we worked on the night before. When he made the same mistake three times in a row, I found myself saying sternly, "John, think! Sound out the word! A-s-t-r-o-n-a-u-t. We did this just last night and you knew it then."

John's eyes welled up, and he looked panicked and desperate. Though I hadn't intended to spoil his breakfast or his confidence, I did. That's what impatience can do to a child. It doesn't matter that I felt tired and pressured by the clock. What John knows is that I lost my patience.

A recent study by York University revealed that patience topped the list of skills parents thought they needed most. What's more, impatience was the number one attitude they did not want to pass on to their children.[1]

It's not a big surprise, really. Patience, according to many experts, is one of the most important traits a parent can master in raising kids. Why? Because first of all, kids are experts at trying their parents' patience—whether they mean to or not. And second, it's all too easy to lose our patience as parents. With one quick snap of annoyance, we can say or do something we soon regret.

So how important is patience to parenting? Let's put it this way: It's impossible to be a loving parent without an abundance of patience. Maybe that's why Paul begins his famous love poem of 1 Corinthians 13 with it: "Love is patient."

Young children are trying to figure out their world, their abilities, and the people around them. Their budding skills, whether physical or emotional, are much slower and more immature than an adult's. They can have a difficult time understanding what adults expect of them, and they can also experience frustration when they can't quite do what they expect of their own small bodies. The result is a season ripe for frustration and impatience. Even as young children are learning new skills, parents often have to fight the urge to help them put the puzzle piece in the right spot or finish a sentence for them. And that's exactly why patience—whether it's in the face of crying babies, toddler meltdowns, school-age sloppiness, or preteen defiance—is every loving parent's priority. It's why patience, as the saying goes, is a virtue.

A Self-Test: How Patient Are You?

The following true/false self-test is designed to get your wheels turning. Don't worry about trying to get the "right" answer; just give the answer that lines up with what you currently believe.

T   F   No matter how "under control" a parent might be, some children are certain to cause a parent to "lose it."

T F   Patience has more to do with a parent's focus than a child's behavior.

T F   If you give a child a warning and he continues a behavior against your will, you have a right to "lose your patience."

T F   It's the child's job to learn to see the world from the parent's point of view — more than it is the parent's job to see it from the child's.

T F   Patience has more to do with the present than with the future.

Scoring: If you answered "true" to any of these five items, you will benefit from brushing up on how to be patient with your child. Even if you answered "false" to each of these items, you can always learn new ways to become more patient.

How to Become a Patient Parent

From one of the great dynasties in China comes an apocryphal story of a wise man who experienced extraordinary relationships. He got along with everyone. He never argued with friends or family members. His children were extremely kind and polite. He enjoyed remarkable harmony in and out of his home.

News of this insightful man traveled to the Chinese emperor, who became so impressed by this man's relational acuity that he ordered the man to write a great scroll describing how others could produce such outstanding relationships with friends and family. The emperor declared by royal proclamation that the scroll was to contain ten thousand words.

> Sometimes parenting can be like bungee jumping: you don't know what will happen until you reach the end of your rope!
>
> **George D. Rose**

57

The man was sent off to write. Days later he delivered a heavy scroll to the emperor's palace. The scroll was immediately taken to the great hall, where it was rolled out across a huge table. The emperor began to read as observers stood silent. After a few minutes, the emperor slowly nodded his approval as the onlookers breathed a sigh of relief.

As requested, the man had written ten thousand words—actually, he had written the same word again and again: *Patience. Patience. Patience.*

Few would disagree with the power of patience. Its value is indisputable. But how can you, as a sometimes pressured and frazzled parent, hold on to patience when you feel as if you're about to lose it all? Let's start with the most obvious answer.

Patient Parents Stay Cool and Calm

It almost goes without saying. But not quite. If you are to keep from reacting with impatience and frustration, you must remain calm. Of course, keeping your cool is much easier said than done. So what's an irritated parent to do? Try the old technique of counting to ten? Perhaps, but we can do better than that.

> Patience is a bitter plant, but it bears sweet fruit.
>
> **German proverb**

Jon Kabat-Zinn, founder of the Stress Reduction Clinic at the Massachusetts Medical Center and coauthor of *Everyday Blessings: The Inner Work of Mindful Parenting*, suggests that if we practice mindfulness—the art of bringing our full attention to bear on the moment at hand—we can't help but remain cool and calm even if we are at the end of our rope.[2]

Let's get specific. We lose our patience with a dawdling six-year-old on the way to school because mentally we're already sifting through the papers on our desk at work.

In other words, we aren't being mindful in the moment. You see, patience is a choice. You choose to pay attention in a very focused way because you know it's important—for example, you wait by the door while your preschooler struggles to tie his shoes because you know that mastering this skill will help him gain confidence. But you don't have to wait forever. You can scoop up your child and his shoes and tell him, "It's time for us to go now," without losing your patience and getting angry.

Patient Parents Guard Against Justifying Their Impatience

Peggy Carlson tells about her three-year-old son's experience in Sunday school one morning. The teacher mentioned to Peggy that it had been a wild morning—the children just wouldn't settle down. Peggy's son, Clayton, was one of the culprits. When the teacher said to him, "Clayton, come and sit down on the rug, pronto," Clayton indignantly replied, "Nobody calls me Pronto!"

> Our patience will achieve more than our force.
>
> **Edmund Burke**

Ever felt like Clayton? Nobody likes to be bossed around. Yet think of all the times we as parents boss our kids around when we're running low on patience. We bark orders and snap commands. "You get over here immediately!" But worse than bossing is when we set up a scenario that attempts to justify our impatience with our child. "If you don't finish that food on your plate in the next two minutes, I am going to lose it. I'm not kidding!" Or we might even say, "I'm warning you!" as if we now have permission to lose our temper because we said we would.

This last approach is perhaps the most telling sign that a "patient" parent is not so patient at all. If you find yourself resorting to these tactics, you must give them up. They do nothing but teach your child that getting angry is okay as long as you tell people you're about to blow your stack.

Patient Parents Understand a Child's Perspective

In 1997, Reeve Lindbergh, daughter of aviator Charles Lindbergh, was invited to give the annual Lindbergh Address at the Smithsonian Institution's Air and Space Museum to commemorate the seventieth anniversary of her father's historic solo flight across the Atlantic. On the day of the speech, museum officials invited her to come early, before the facility opened, so that she could have a close-up look at the *Spirit of St. Louis*, the little plane suspended from the museum ceiling that her father had piloted from New York to Paris in 1927.

That morning in the museum, Reeve and her young son, Ben, eagerly climbed into the bucket of a cherry picker, a long-armed crane that carried them upward until the plane was at eye level and within their reach. Seeing the machine that her father had so bravely flown across the sea was an unforgettable experience for Reeve. She had never touched the plane before, and that morning, twenty feet above the floor of the museum, she tenderly reached out to run her fingers along the door handle, which she knew her father must have grasped many times with his own hand.

> They also serve who only stand and wait.
>
> **John Milton**

Tears welled up in her eyes at the thought of what she was doing. "Oh, Ben," she whispered, her voice trembling, "isn't this amazing?"

"Yeaaaah," Ben replied, equally impressed. "I've never been in a cherry picker before!"

Now, how would you react if you were Reeve Lindbergh enjoying this extremely special and unprecedented moment? It would be tempting to scold your young son, wouldn't it? After all, he's missing the point of the whole experience. But that's normal for most kids—

they aren't seeing the world as adults. As parents, we might find that reality tough to handle. We have to beware that our expectations for our kids' behavior might be out of line with what they're capable of developmentally.

It all comes down to adjusting our expectations. A toddler in an itchy tux at a family wedding, for example, isn't going to be able to sit through the after-dinner speeches happily. And if you expect him to, you'll end up in a vicious circle of misery. You've set yourself up for losing your patience.

Patient Parents Practice Longsuffering

"I want to carry my banjo with me," asserted our son John, then five.

We were preparing to take a long walk around a lake not far from our house when he decided that he'd like to strap on a plastic play instrument that was nearly as big as he was.

"John, that's not a good idea, buddy. You'll get tired of carrying it very quickly, and then Daddy or I will have to carry it for you," I said while kneeling down to talk eye to eye.

"No, I want to carry it the whole way by myself," John insisted.

"Honey, it's just not going to work."

"Yes, it is," he protested.

I could feel myself growing impatient as this dialogue continued for several minutes. Finally, I said, "Okay, John, here's the deal. You can carry your banjo on this walk, but I want you to remember something."

John, sensing he had won this little victory, nodded in agreement.

"If you decide after all this protesting that you no longer want to carry your banjo once we start our walk, you have to agree that the next time you ask to do something that Mommy or Daddy says is not a good idea, you will go along with what we say. Okay?"

John agreed and had his banjo strung over his shoulder in no time flat.

Needless to say, John soon saw the folly of his decision, and the deal we made with him before the walk may have been one of the best things we've done to get him to respect our influence. Even to this day, three years later, we can say, "Remember the banjo incident?" and he will almost always readily respect our input. But it took a bit of longsuffering. We had to calmly endure a circumstance — admittedly not terribly painful but bothersome nonetheless — that we knew we could have avoided if we'd been less patient and just run over his immature desire.

It's not surprising that some translations of 1 Corinthians 13 say something to the effect of "Love suffereth long" in place of "Love is patient." After all, patience is measured by our ability to endure something we'd rather not. Each of us is destined to suffer if we aspire to be patient. But we don't have to suffer as passive victims. Love suffers long not because its strength is in endurance but because its power is in the future. Love empowers patience, for example, to care for a troubled teen and see that brighter days are ahead.

Love is patient. And just as our patience is almost exhausted, love empowers us to find a little more.

For Discussion

1. On a scale of 1 to 10, how would you rank the importance of being a patient parent? Why?

2. On that same scale, how would you rank your natural inclination to be patient with your child?

3. In specific terms, when are you most likely to lose your patience with your child? Name the place or conditions. How does your impatience manifest itself? (What do you say or do that conveys impatience to your child?)

4. When is the next time your child is likely to try your patience? What can you do now to prepare for this situation?

CHAPTER 6

Hearing What They Don't Say: Are You an *Attentive* Parent?

A mother understands
what a child does not say.
Jewish proverb

Jackson, our three-year-old, is a talker. He can tell you how to avoid stepping into the imaginary "hot lava" he always jumps around in our living room, for example. He can tell you that Davey Crockett wore a "fancy hat." He can tell you that the answer to nearly any addition problem that he hears his older brother trying to solve is "six" — whether it's 8 + 2 or 5 + 4. But most of all, Jackson can ask questions. Lots of questions:

"Is silver a color?"

"Why do they call it golf?"

"Do worms have ears?"

"How come Harper (our cat) doesn't get burned in the hot lava?"

Jackson has more questions than we have answers. (If you don't believe us, just spend an hour with him in the backseat of your car while you're doing errands.) And for the most part, we love his questions. But every once in a while, when we don't quickly reply or we're too preoccupied with something else to give an immediate response, Jack will pose a question that hangs in silence. And, as if he's just delivered a joke that bombed in a New York comedy club, he'll say with a rise in his voice, "Anybody?"

It makes us laugh every time.

We laugh, primarily, because we know just how he feels. Haven't you sometimes wondered if anyone out there is listening? We all know the feeling—but not all of us have the compunction to blurt out, "Anyone?"

> The most important thing in communication is to hear what isn't being said.
>
> **Peter Drucker**

Our eight-year-old, John, doesn't. He isn't as chatty as his younger brother. In fact, sometimes we have to work vigilantly just to get John to open up. If we don't, he can be content to process his day internally, without saying much. But even Jack, with all his verbalizing, doesn't necessarily say what we need to understand. That's why we work hard to be attentive to both of our boys.

Chances are, you're the same way with your children—on the lookout for any clues of what's going on beneath the surface. In a word, you're attentive. But if you're like a lot of parents who need to be sure they're keeping this practice in play, we devote this chapter to you.

ATTENTIVE ATTENTIVE ATTENTIVE ATTENTIVE ATTENTIVE ATTENTIVE ATTENTIVE ATTENTIVE ATTENTIVE ATTENTIVE

What does it mean to be attentive? Quite simply, it means to give attention. Well, of course, right? But "giving attention" is more profound than you might first guess. A person who is attentive is mindful. He considerately sees to the comfort or wishes of another. He's thoughtful and watchful, looking for ways to give care. He attends to details—little nonverbal behaviors that may speak more honestly than words. As the dictionary makes clear, to be attentive means "to express affectionate interest through close observation and gallant gestures."

Wow! Gallant gestures! Don't you like that? It means that if you are to be attentive, you need to be brave. The gallant person goes where others may fear to travel. And that's exactly what the attentive parent does. She explores uncharted territory with her child. It's uncharted, as we are about to see, because we don't know where it will lead. But we do know that deeper connections with our children are always the result whenever we take an attentive journey.

The Undeniable Importance of Being an Attentive Parent

From the moment of birth, children cry out for attention — literally. But as they become preschoolers and grade-schoolers, and then high school kids and college-age young adults, their requests for attention become much more sophisticated. As a parent, you'll need to become adept at deciphering exactly what they are saying. Sometimes it's found in the subtleties of nonverbal behavior. At other times it's apparent in the bigger actions they take. For example, a preschooler may seek attention by throwing a tantrum or hitting his sibling. A fourth grader may seek attention by getting in trouble at school. A fifteen-year-old may seek attention by starting to smoke. You get the idea. Kids don't advertise the fact that they need your attention. They want you to give it without their having to ask. And if you aren't deciphering their coded requests, they'll become more and more drastic — until they stop asking for your attention altogether.

Allow us to say it straight: If your child doesn't receive the personalized attention she craves, she will eventually disengage and write

> Be quick to listen,
> slow to speak.
>
> **James 1:19**

you off as irrelevant. We know this may sound harsh, but it's true. If a child does not receive the attention that only her parent can give, she'll find that attentiveness somewhere else — typically from her peers. And, coincidentally, it will happen right about the time she becomes eligible for her driver's permit.

A Self-Test: How Attentive Are You?

The following true/false self-test is designed to get your wheels turning. Don't worry about trying to get the "right" answer; just give the answer that lines up with what you currently believe.

T   F   One of the best ways to handle a child's anger is to ignore it.

T   F   If something really matters to my child, she'll say so.

T   F   It's nearly impossible to accurately identify a child's thoughts and feelings if he doesn't express them.

T   F   If my child has a problem, she almost always wants me to help her solve it.

T   F   If you validate the feelings of a child's irrational fear, you reinforce illogical reasoning.

Scoring: If you answered "true" to any of these five items, you will benefit from brushing up on how to be attentive to your child. Even if you answered "false" to each of these items, you can always learn new ways to become more attentive.

How to Become an Attentive Parent

At the heart of cultivating attentiveness is your capacity to "listen with the third ear." Hearing what your child isn't saying is paramount to being an attentive parent. Every parent can hear the words a child speaks, but the attentive parent goes beneath the surface to listen for the emotions, values, fears, and pains that aren't overtly expressed. Let's explore how to do just that and more.

Attentive Parents Listen for a Child's Emotions

Every child is a unique book a parent needs to read. We can't assume we know what our kids are feeling if we haven't studied them carefully. When you listen to your child with the "third ear," it's as if you are panning for gold. Just as a miner sifts through sand and pebbles to find a golden nugget, your job as an attentive parent is to sift through your child's communication (including nonverbal clues) and lift out the nugget of emotion. Hold it carefully, then hand it back to your child, saying, "Here, is this how you feel?"

> The first duty of love is to listen.
>
> **Paul Tillich**

We can't overstate the value of mastering the skill of listening for your child's feelings. Few things will open your child's heart more to you. Few things will endear you more to them. When you listen with the third ear, you not only hear the emotions your child isn't saying but also help him put those emotions into words. Here's an example of this skill at work in the life of Justin, a thirteen-year-old who refuses to do his homework.

Justin: I don't care what you or the school wants to do to me. I'm not going to do another assignment for that teacher.

Mom: *(Restraining her desire to lay down the law)* Sounds as if you've made up your mind.

Justin: Yep. Mr. Wilson is an idiot. They shouldn't even allow him to be at that school.

Mom: He's not too smart, huh?

Justin: Well, I'm sure he's smart and everything, but he isn't very nice.

69

Mom: He's treated you kind of mean?

Justin: Yeah. The last time I handed in my paper, Wilson read it out loud. I didn't write that for the whole world to hear.

Mom: You felt betrayed.

Justin: Exactly! What would you do if you were me?

Can you put yourself in the place of this mother? Consider the restraint that you, as a parent, must have to muster up this kind of empathy and listen for feelings. Remember from our earlier definition of *attentive* that this trait requires gallant bravery. But also notice the reward that results from attentive listening. Once you've accurately identified your child's emotions with a caring attitude, his spirit opens up almost instantaneously.

Attentive Parents Listen for a Child's Values

German theologian Helmut Thielicke describes the experience of hearing a child raise a "frightful cry" because he had shoved his hand into the opening of a very expensive Chinese vase but couldn't pull it out. Parents and neighbors tugged with might on the poor child's arm as he howled out loud. Finally, there was nothing left to do but to break the beautiful, costly vase. "And then as the mournful heap of shards lay there," says Thielicke, "it became clear why the child had been so hopelessly stuck. His little fist grasped a paltry penny which he had spied in the bottom of the vase and which he, in his childish ignorance, would not let go."[1]

This well-known story illustrates the powerful need to listen carefully to our children's values. Had the adults in this story tried to understand why the child's hand was in a fist, they happily could have explained how the child could achieve his goal without sacrificing the valuable vase. In the same way, as an attentive parent, you can avoid costly arguments and conflict with your child by paying careful attention to what she values.

Recently our little Jackson refused to take a vitamin we'd set on his dinner plate. "I don't want to take this vitamin," he wailed. Our first instinct was to force the issue and fulfill our "parental authority." Instead, we asked, "You don't want to take your vitamin today?"

"No, I don't want this one—I want my Scooby-Doo vitamin."

And that was that. Problem solved. Instead of reacting to what we initially read as resistance, we simply heard him out and discovered what mattered to him.

Of course, as children grow older and enter the teenage years, this kind of listening becomes even more important to the attentive parent. A teenager's values can test your gallant bravery, but if you sincerely and continually uncover what your child values— whether it be a particular video game, a certain brand of perfume, or a type of music—as a way to understand your child's heart, you'll have a direct line to his or her world. And while a teenager's values are sure to surprise you, remember that if you don't know about them, you don't stand a chance of influencing them. So listen attentively, restraining judgment until your child is sure you fully understand.

> A good listener is not only popular everywhere, but after a while he gets to know something.
> **Wilson Mizner**

Attentive Parents Listen for a Child's Fears

Parents can be quick to discount a child's irrational fear. We tell them, for example, that it's silly to be afraid of the dark. We discount their social anxiety and tell them to speak up and be friendlier. As adults, we stand on the platform of experience that tends to drive our discounting ways. But each time we readily dismiss our kids' fears, we invalidate a piece of our kids themselves.

Attentive parents, of course, take a different route. With listening ears, they work to understand the source of a child's fears in order to soothe them. We recently read about the young Teddy Roosevelt and his mother, whom he called "Mittie." She had found that he was so afraid of the Madison Square Church in New York that he refused to set foot inside it alone. He was terrified, she discovered, of something called the "zeal." Teddy feared it was crouched in the dark corners of the church, ready to jump out at him. When his mother asked what a zeal might be, young Teddy said he wasn't sure but thought it was probably a large animal or perhaps a dragon. He told her he'd heard the minister read about it from the Bible. Using a concordance, his mother read him those passages containing the word *zeal* until suddenly, excitedly, Teddy told her to stop. The line was from the book of John: "And his disciples remembered that it was written, The zeal of thine house hath eaten me up."

> Well-timed silence hath more eloquence than speech.
>
> **Martin Farquhar Tupper**

Patiently, tenderly, attentively, Roosevelt's mother listened to understand and appreciate his fear. She didn't say, "Teddy, you're acting silly — quit being afraid of nothing."

When you resist the urge to discount your child's fear and instead try to understand the root of the fear, you will soon discover another part of your child's heart — and, in turn, your child will grow closer to yours.

Attentive Parents Listen for a Child's Pain

A close cousin to your child's fear is his pain. All of us have aches and hurts we don't express — and they typically come out through hysterics and aggressive fits. The attentive parent taps into these tantrums with sensitive ears.

Triple-platinum rapper and producer Eminem is known for his violent, controversial lyrics. He vents on everything from his unhappy childhood in a single-parent home to his contempt for various celebrities and the mainstream media. His songs frequently defame others, including his family members.

For example, Eminem claims in his raps that his mother is welfare dependent and a drug addict and that she sleeps around. He calls her a horrible mother and says he hopes she burns in hell. But his mother, Debbie Nelson, doesn't take his words to heart: "That's just artistic expression," she says. "He's very sad on the inside. He is hurting a lot. And I can see it. I can see through my son. I know him like the back of my hand."[2]

We don't know a thing about Debbie Nelson, but this response to her son certainly bears the marks of attentiveness. Every parent who can see beneath layers of anger or aggressiveness to recognize a child's pain has tremendous courage. Many a parent can respond to a child's rage by matching it with even more rage, though such retaliation is never productive. A thoughtful, caring ear will accomplish far more than any attempts to lash out.

> Attend with the ear of your heart.
>
> **St. Benedict**

When I was seven or so, I (Les) threw terrible tantrums for a short season. I can remember them clearly even now as an adult. But even more memorable is my parents' response to them. While setting up boundaries and consequences for my behavior, they didn't neglect to understand my feelings. Through attentive listening, they soon discovered the pain I felt in having to repeat first grade. While all my buddies were moving on to second grade, I was being held back. To an average adult, my dilemma may not have seemed very painful, but I'm thankful my parents were attentive to just how tender this hurt was.

Attentive Parents Listen for Ways to Express Affection

Steve Harmon is one of the most attentive dads we know. Though we had known Steve and Jewell for many years, we didn't realize how attentive Steve was to his daughters until one of them, Chelsea, became a freshman in one of our university classes. A few weeks into the semester, Steve phoned our office and asked if he could bring a dozen roses to Chelsea at the beginning of one class that week. It was her birthday.

We happily agreed, and Steve showed up with roses in hand. He unpretentiously came down the aisle of the auditorium and handed the bouquet to his daughter. "Happy birthday, Chelsea," he said quietly; then he left the room as quickly as he'd entered. Chelsea was grinning from ear to ear. And the more than one hundred students looking on spontaneously applauded. Chelsea then revealed that her dad had been bringing her flowers on her birthday since she was in grade school. With this news, a chorus of "ohhs" arose from many of the female students.

Do you think this young woman feels affection from her father? Without a doubt. Attentive parents study their children to find countless ways to show affection.

For Discussion

1. On a scale of 1 to 10, how would you rank the importance of being an attentive parent? Why?

2. On that same scale, how would you rank your natural inclination to hear what your child doesn't say?

3. In specific terms, note some recent examples of when you were tuned in and attentive to your child. How do you know?

4. When are the most important times for you to be attentive to your child — times when it is especially challenging for you to be tuned in? What makes these times challenging, and what can you do to prepare for them?

CHAPTER 7

Seeing a Picture of Their Future: Are You a *Visionary* Parent?

A child is not a vase to be filled,
but a fire to be lit.
François Rabelais

On my (Les's) thirteenth birthday, Mom and Dad gave me a present that was better than I even hoped for. It was a drafting table — complete with a big ribbon tied around it and all the drafting tools I could want. For the better part of a year, I'd been talking about how I wanted to be an architect. I'm not sure where I got the idea or why I wanted to pursue it, but it was my dream — that is, if I didn't make it in the NBA playing for the Boston Celtics!

So Mom and Dad caught the vision. But it didn't end with the table. The next week, Dad got permission from my eighth grade teacher to take me out of class for the day so I could visit the University of Illinois School of Architecture with him. He'd made a couple of appointments so that I could talk with some of the officials, and Dad and I made a day of it.

That night over dinner, we filled Mom in on our adventure. I was animated with excitement. In the weeks and months that followed, Mom or Dad would put a clipping on my desk that pertained to something architectural that they thought I'd find interesting. One weekend Mom took me on a tour of Frank Lloyd Wright's famous homes near Chicago. Both of my parents invested in my dream and helped me shape a vision of what I might do with my life.

Needless to say, I didn't become an architect. That dream started to fade a couple of years later after I took my first course in psychology. But that didn't matter. The point is, Mom and Dad were, and still are, visionary parents — helping me see what my future might entail and showing me what it would take to make my dreams a reality.

> Vision is the art of seeing things invisible.
>
> **Jonathan Swift**

Helen Keller was once asked, "What would be worse than being born blind?" She answered, "To have sight without vision." Every visionary parent understands this sentiment. And every child who is blessed with a visionary parent has wings.

VISIONARY

A dictionary will tell you that *visionary* means "characterized by vision or foresight." It will also tell you that a visionary is a person with a clear, distinctive, and specific picture of the future, usually connected with advances in technology or political arrangements. One dictionary we consulted gives Steve Jobs, founder of Apple Computer, as an example of a visionary. He's a man who could envision a technological development that few other people on the planet saw coming.

When applied to parenthood, the concept of vision has to do with parents who can see a potential picture of their child's future. Though careful not to impose their own picture on a child, they study their child's gifts, uniqueness, and dreams to catch a glimpse of what life could be for their child. In other words, they help a child raise her sights for the future and capture a personal vision that will give her hope and passion in the present.

The Undeniable Importance of Being a Visionary Parent

Without vision, the Bible says, people perish. Vision is essential to a life well lived because vision almost always ensures passion. When we have no vision, our zest for living dies and we wander, zombie-like, through our existence.

Parents who help a child capture a vision are, by default, helping that child become determined and persistent. "Burning desire to be or do something gives us staying power," says educator and author, Marsha Sinetar. She's talking about enthusiasm, fervor, zeal. She's talking about passion. And you can mark her words—passion propels persistence. It's what enables a child to pick himself up and start in again after a defeat. Why is passion important? Because every great vision is fraught with disappointments and setbacks along the way.

Another value that visionary parents bring to their child is discipline. Think about it. Every achiever, every visionary who aspires to greatness, is asked again and again, "Where do you get your energy? How do you get so many things done?" People are amazed that one person can accomplish so much. They ask these questions because they feel that high achievers must have a secret to their productivity; they must know something others don't. If there's any secret, it's found in a single word: *vision.*

Vision stirs passions that in turn compel a maturing child to prioritize what she does. She hardly has to work at it. People with passion rarely need help to prioritize their time because passion does it for them. Can you imagine Pablo Picasso dragging himself into his painting studio and forcing himself to paint because it was on his schedule?

Of course not. The image is absurd. He couldn't help but paint. It was his passion. If anything, he had to force himself to eat because his painting would consume him for hours on end.

> The future belongs to those who believe in the beauty of their dreams.
>
> **Eleanor Roosevelt**

Our friends George and Arlys have a daughter in high school who is passionate about rowing. Hanna wakes up at 5:30 most mornings to join her rowing team as they train for state finals. And, you guessed it, George and Arlys are with her every step of the way, because they are visionary parents who see the value her vision has in building discipline, persistence, and maturity.

A Self-Test: How Visionary Are You?

The following true/false self-test is designed to get your wheels turning. Don't worry about trying to get the "right" answer; just give the answer that lines up with what you currently believe.

- T   F   I have several strong ideas about what my child should do when she grows older.
- T   F   I'm not very concerned about seeing the future for my child. All that matters is being fully present right now.
- T   F   Having a vision for my child's future is very low on my priority list as a parent.
- T   F   It's up to my child to eventually find his own vision for his life. My goal is to remain hands-off until he discovers it and then be supportive.

T   F   I may not have a vision for myself, but I can still help my
child capture a personal vision for the future.

Scoring: If you answered "true" to any of these five items, you will
benefit from brushing up on how to be visionary for your child. Even
if you answered "false" to each of these items, you can always learn
new ways to become more visionary.

How to Become a Visionary Parent

We've long enjoyed hearing what happened when Disney World first
opened in Florida. Since Walt had passed away, Mrs. Disney was
asked to speak at the grand opening. She was introduced by a man
who said, "Mrs. Disney, I just wish Walt could have seen this." She
stepped up to the podium and said, "He did." Then she sat down.

And she's right. Walt saw it long before anyone else because he
had a clear vision. So how do parents go about seeing a picture of
their child's future? And how can they do so without imposing their
own vision on their child? It starts, in our opinion, with prayer.

Visionary Parents Pray
for Their Child's Future

Erwin McManus, the catalyst behind Awaken, a collaboration of
dreamers committed to creating environments that expand imagina-
tion and unleash creativity, tells the story of when his son, Aaron,
became frightened at youth camp. He was just a little guy when some
of the camp personnel told stories about demons and Satan. When
Aaron returned home, he was still terrified.

"Dad, don't turn off the light!" he said before going to bed. "Daddy,
could you stay here with me? Daddy, I'm afraid. They told all these
stories about demons."

Erwin regretted sending him to the camp.

"Daddy, Daddy, would you pray for me that I would be safe?"

Erwin said to his son, "Aaron, I will not pray for you to be safe. I will pray that God will make you dangerous, so dangerous that demons will flee when you enter the room."

"All right," Aaron said. "But pray I would be really, really dangerous, Daddy."

Erwin knew he was praying not only for his son's immediate circumstances but for his future as well. He was praying that Aaron would grow up to be a man who doesn't fear but rather stands strong and courageous. And that's the kind of prayer every visionary parent prays.

We pray God will teach us how to be better visionaries for John and Jack. We pray God will make a picture of their futures clearer and clearer as they age. We pray each of our boys will embody traits that will serve them well as they grow into manhood and discover their callings.

And just recently, we began praying for the kinds of husbands they will be—and for the little girls out there whom they may marry. In fact, we got the idea to pray for their future this way at a wedding we recently attended. At the reception, the bride's dad gave an eloquent speech, telling the guests that he and his wife had been praying since Julie was a baby, not only for her future, but for the man she would marry one day—the boy who would become the man who would one day become their daughter's husband.

> If one advances confidently in the direction of one's dreams, and endeavors to live the life which one has imagined, one will meet with a success unexpected in common hours.
>
> **Henry David Thoreau**

We also learned recently from a friend that she and her husband write their prayers for their three children in three journals they keep near their bedside. Not only are the journals tangible reminders to pray for their kids, but they serve as a priceless treasure of blessing that they'll give to each of their children one day. Talk about being visionary!

Visionary Parents Picture a Special Future for Their Child

Sidel, a young Jewish mother, was proudly walking down the street pushing a stroller containing her infant twins. As she rounded the corner, she encountered her neighbor Sarah. "My, what beautiful children," Sarah cooed. "What are their names?"

Pointing to each child, Sidel replied, "This is Bennie, the doctor, and Reuben, the lawyer."

Jewish homes have had a long history of picturing special futures for their children. In the Old Testament, Isaac prophesied that his son Jacob would be a strong leader (see Genesis 27:28–29). And Jacob, as a grown man, prophesied about the future of his sons. But don't worry — you don't have to be a prophet to picture a special future for your child. You can't predict his future with biblical accuracy. But you can encourage your child and help him imagine his potential. When a child feels in his heart that the future is hopeful and that Mom and Dad believe in what he can become, he faces life with a strong optimism.

You picture a special future for your child when you say things like, "You have such a generous spirit, I wouldn't be surprised if you end up helping a lot of people when you grow older." Or "You're so helpful around the house, I bet you're going to make a great husband [or wife] to the person you marry someday." Or "You enjoy studying the ocean so much, I wonder if you might be a marine biologist someday."

These are ways of planting little seeds that may or may not take root. The point is, as a visionary parent, you are considering your child's future. You aren't imparting your own egocentric vision of what you want your child to become. You are sensitive to your child's unique gifts and qualities, and you point them out on occasion to highlight how they could be maximized in the future.

> If you raise your children to feel that they can accomplish any goal or task they decide upon, you will have succeeded as a parent and you will have given your children the greatest of all blessings.
> **Brian Tracy**

Visionary Parents Have a Vision for Themselves

A law in physics says that water cannot rise above its source. The same is true, in a sense, for your child. If you don't have a vision for yourself, your child will have that much more difficulty rising to any vision that you might help him capture. For parents to be truly effective in seeing a picture of their child's future, they must have a picture for themselves. Why? Because being visionary isn't something that is done only for others. It must be modeled.

Becoming more visionary may be a struggle for some. My (Leslie's) book *You Matter More Than You Think* contains a chapter titled "Dream Venti." It's about dreaming a big dream for your life — and I receive more notes and emails from women on this chapter than on anything else I've ever written. So many moms tell me they have put their dreams on the back burner while raising their kids. I understand that. But your kids need to see that you have dreams too.

I think that's why I like the true story of baseball player Jim Morris, who is played by Dennis Quaid in the movie *The Rookie*. The movie depicts how Morris, whose minor league pitching career ended with a shoulder injury, begins coaching high school baseball as a way to be involved in the game he loves. The team, recognizing Jim's talent, makes a deal with him. If they win the district championship, then the coach must try out for the major leagues. The team wins the title, and Jim has to follow through on a deal he never imagined he would have to keep.

The initial reaction of his wife, Lorri, is negative. The couple experience several tense moments as they wrestle with the decision. One evening as Lorri tucks their eight-year-old son into bed, she is reminded that Hunter is his dad's biggest fan.

Lorri joins her husband on the porch.

Jim asks, "Kids down?"

"For a while at least," she replies.

Jim apologizes for the tension between the two of them and then shares his willingness to let go of the baseball opportunity. But Lorri has experienced a change of heart.

She says, "We've got an eight-year-old boy inside this house who waited all day in the sun and the rain to see his daddy try to do something that nobody believed he could do. Now, what are we telling him if you don't try now?"

> We go where our vision is.
> **Joseph Murphy**

Inspired, Jim Morris goes on to amaze scouts with the speed of his fastball, and despite his age, he receives a major league contract. But most important, he gives his son a model of dreaming to emulate.

We'll say it again: Visionary parents have a vision for themselves.

Visionary Parents Impart Their Blessing

In 1986 our friends Gary Smalley and John Trent wrote a book titled *The Blessing* that became an instant bestseller. Thousands of people identified with its message of receiving a blessing from their parents and passing on that blessing to their children. What is "the blessing"? It's the knowledge that someone in the world loves and accepts you unconditionally. And that's exactly what you give your child when you picture a special future for him. According to Gary and John, seeing a special future for a child is like building him a campfire on a dark night. It draws him "toward the warmth of genuine concern and fulfilled potential — instead of leaving a child to head into a dark unknown."[1]

So as you light a pathway for your child's future, don't neglect the importance of giving your child the blessing of unconditional love and acceptance. Painter Benjamin West is a good example of someone who received this blessing as a child. He tells how he loved to paint as a youngster. One day when his mother left the house, he pulled out all the paints and made quite a mess. He hoped to get it cleaned up before his mother came back, but she returned before he was finished and discovered the mess. West explains that what she did next completely surprised him. She picked up his painting and said, "My, what a beautiful painting of your sister." Then she gave him a kiss on the cheek and walked away. With that kiss, West says, he became a painter.

Every day you have the opportunity to paint a picture of the future for your child — even when it seems they've made a mess. And each time you apply a single stroke to this picture, you are giving an immeasurable blessing.

For Discussion

1. On a scale of 1 to 10, how would you rank the importance of being a visionary parent? Why?

1   2   3   4   5   6   7   8   9   10

2. On that same scale, how would you rank your natural inclination to see a picture of your child's future? On what evidence do you base your ranking?

1   2   3   4   5   6   7   8   9   10

3. In specific terms, when did you most recently help your child picture a special future? What did you do, and how did your child respond?

4. When is the next time you are likely to have an opportunity to cast a vision for your child? What can you do now to maximize the opportunity?

CHAPTER 8

Building a Better Bond: Are You a *Connected* Parent?

*To be in your children's memories tomorrow,
you have to be in their lives today.*
Anonymous

Donut dates. That's what my mom and I called them. Starting when I (Leslie) was in the sixth grade, my mom initiated a standing appointment with me each week at the neighborhood donut shop. We met there nearly every week until I left home for college. We didn't have an agenda. We didn't study a book together, review homework, or do anything like that. We just talked about whatever was going on that week—which usually involved relationships. And Mom always listened. She didn't jump in to solve problems or give advice without my asking. Looking back, I realize what an amazing gift these times with my mom were. She was a busy pastor's wife, and I know she made our donut date a top priority when she had plenty of other activities that could have crowded it out. And to this day our connection runs deep.

Like Leslie, I (Les) had a good model of how to be a connected parent. My dad would order the textbooks I was reading in school so that we could discuss them together. But our discussions were more than academic. The books were merely a springboard for other meaningful connections. In fact, as a sophomore in high school, I did research on the Oregon Trail and wrote a fairly lengthy paper on it. One day Dad and I were discussing the amazing wagon trains that made this passage, when we both came to the same conclusion: "Let's follow the trail this summer." I don't know which one of us said it first, but that's exactly what we did. We took ten days, just the two of us, to drive from Independence, Missouri, to the mouth of the Columbia River, stopping at every point of special interest to us along the way. I'll never forget it. And the connection we forged then has endured to this day.

> Kids learn our values when they feel free to ask questions.
>
> **Janice Crouse**

Maybe it's because of the models we had growing up that both of us are committed to building strong bonds with our boys. Chances are, you feel the same desire to connect with your children. This chapter is dedicated to helping you do just that. We begin, as usual, by discovering exactly what it means to be "connected."

Look up the word *connect*, and you'll quickly see it has several meanings. The one we're concerned with has to do with establishing rapport or relationship. Connected parents build a bond or link with their child. How? Primarily through *communication*—a word that isn't far removed in its origin from "connect." That's precisely why you hear people say, "Let's connect." They mean, "Let's talk."

Our English word *communication* comes from the Latin *communis*, which means "common." Makes sense, doesn't it? We are most connected when we find we have something in common with another person. The same is true in a parent-child relationship. Parents who connect find ways to identify with their child. Why? Because when you have something in common, you join your hearts. You stand on common ground.

The Undeniable Importance of Being a Connected Parent

Dr. Nick Stinnett is one of the nation's leading clinical researchers in identifying what makes strong families. Beginning at Oklahoma State University and continuing at the University of Nebraska, Stinnett and his colleagues have compiled the largest database on strong families in the world.

After interviewing thousands of successful families, Stinnett and his associates have isolated six consistent marks of what he terms a "fantastic family." The number one mark of such a family is that the parents choose to make an unconditional commitment to each child. In Stinnett's words, "Members of strong families are dedicated to promoting each other's welfare and happiness. They express their commitment to one another—not just in words, but through choosing to invest time and energy. Their commitment to each other is active and obvious."[1]

> The best inheritance a parent can give to his children is a few minutes of their time each day.
> **M. Grundler**

Showing this kind of commitment is what being a connected parent is all about—and according to research, it's the most important thing you can do for your child. It tops the list! What's more, most parents agree that commitment is an extremely important quality. So you'd think we'd have fantastic families in abundance. Unfortunately, just because parents agree that this quality is important doesn't mean they are putting it into practice. Peter Benson, president of the Search Institute, an independent nonprofit organization whose mission is to promote healthy children, youth, and communities, says, "Relationships are the oxygen of human development. This [Stinnett] study is another attempt to get into the ether of America the notion of the importance of connectedness, the power that real people have but which most of us are not using."

> The bond that links your true family is not one of blood, but of respect and joy in each other's life.
>
> **Richard Bach**

Sad, isn't it? Every parent has the potential to commit to cultivating a meaningful connection, but far too many aren't actually doing so. Does it really matter? You bet! According to a survey conducted by Columbia University's Center on Addiction and Substance Abuse (CASA), "Almost one in five American teens say they live with 'hands-off' adults who fail to consistently set rules and monitor their behavior. These youth are at a four-times greater risk for smoking, drinking, and illegal drug use than their peers with 'hands-on' parents."[2] Studies also show that the more involved adults are in kids' lives, the more likely these kids are to be confident, compassionate, and sociable.

A Self-Test: How Connected Are You?

The following true/false self-test is designed to get your wheels turning. Don't worry about trying to get the "right" answer; just give the answer that lines up with what you currently believe.

T F   I know what my child most often daydreams about.

T F   I know the best and worst part of my child's school day.

T F   I know my child's greatest fear.

T F   I know the names of my child's six closest friends and a little about their parents.

T F I am intentional about having a meaningful conversation
with my child every day.

Scoring: If you answered "false" to any of these five items, you will
benefit from brushing up on how to be more connected to your child.
Even if you answered "true" to each of these items, you can always
learn new ways to become more connected.

How to Become a Connected Parent

The Ledbetters, a family who live not far from us in Seattle, like to
spend time at home — just not in the same room. So they built a
3,600-square-foot house with separate sitting areas for each of their
two children and a master bedroom far from both. The house also includes special rooms for activities such as studying and sewing. Then
there's the escape room, where Mr. Ledbetter says that "any family
member can go to get away from the rest of us."

The Mercer Island, Washington, industrial designer says his seven-
and eleven-year-old daughters now fight less because their new house
gives them so many ways to avoid each other.

Bucking the trend of the open floor plan where domestic life re-
volves around a big central space and an exposed kitchen so that
everyone can connect more easily, this family opted for seclusion.
"It's good for a dysfunctional family," says Gopal
Ahluwahlia, director of research for the National
Association of Home Builders. "All the cut-up
spaces make a family more isolated and lonelier
than ever."[3]

We're betting you, unlike the Ledbetters, want as
much healthy connection with your kids as possible.
So let's take a look at the hallmarks of connected
parents.

> What we're all
> striving for is
> authenticity, a
> spirit-to-spirit
> connection.
> **Oprah Winfrey**

> One important reason to stay calm is that calm parents hear more. Low-key, accepting parents are the ones whose children keep talking.
>
> **Mary Pipher**

Connected Parents Listen So Their Kids Will Talk

Having someone misunderstand you is a lousy experience, whether it be a spouse, a friend, or your boss. When people misunderstand you, they misread you. And if they continue to do so, you won't have any desire to be around them.

Your children feel the same way. Kids who feel consistently misunderstood by Mom or Dad aren't going to approach them. They're going to find someone else to talk to. But when they know they have a parent who understands, or at least wants to understand, you won't be able to keep them away. That's why listening is key.

When you listen to a child, you're subconsciously telling him that he's important. Nothing is more encouraging to a child—preschooler or teenager—than having a parent's undivided attention while speaking.

How do you practice good listening? Let's start with the basics. Look children in the eye when they talk. We don't mean you should stare them down, of course. We mean you should set aside whatever you're doing and make eye contact. If they're toddlers, you should get down on one knee from time to time so you can listen to them at eye level. They'll love you for it.

In our home, with our two boys, we make listening a daily ritual. We have an exercise we call "Mad, Sad, and Glad." Most days, at some point—over dinner, while stuck in traffic, or at bedtime—we'll say, "Let's do Mad, Sad, and Glad." The boys know what that means. First, each of us takes a moment to tell everyone else about one thing that made us mad that day. John, for example, might say, "I got kind of mad when Nathan took the ball from me at recess." We listen attentively and ask follow-up questions. Then we tell about one thing that made us sad. John might say, "I really wanted to check out a library book that Jordan got before me, and that made me a little sad." Again we listen and interact with him. Finally, we share one thing that made us glad. John might say, "I was really glad that we got to go swimming at Grandmother's today."

This little ritual is amazingly simple, but it works wonders for getting children of all ages to open up. To be honest, sometimes we even do this exercise on our own when the kids aren't around. It's a convenient way to listen with the heart on a daily basis.

If you're looking for another practical tool for listening to your kids, start a parent-child journal. Some friends of ours started such a journal with their daughter when she was nine years old. It was actually a mother-daughter journal. One night the daughter would lay it on her mother's nightstand for her to write in. The next night Mom would tuck it under her daughter's pillow for her to record her thoughts and dreams. Through the pages of that little book, they shared secrets, settled arguments, and discussed life. And if journaling fits your child's style, it's guaranteed to let her know you're listening. All you need to do to start a parent-child journal is buy a notebook and write a question to start the conversation. Ask about school, friends, books, or anything else that interests your child. Ask open-ended questions, such as, "Tell me about the best movie you've seen this year." Such questions will help you get more in-depth responses and also communicate that you're all ears.

> Remember: most teens end up being closer to their parents after adolescence than they were before.
>
> **Ron Taffel**

Connected Parents Talk So Their Kids Will Listen

"Hey, pal, how was school?"

"Fine."

"Did you do anything interesting today?"

"Not really."

"Do you want to go out for pizza later?"

"I guess."

Ever had a conversation like this with your child? Almost every parent has. So how can you have quality conversation that consistently engages your child?

It begins with caring. To modify an old adage, your kids don't care how much you know until they know how much you care. It's the same message preached by Jesus in the great Sermon on the Mount: "You're blessed when you care. At the moment of being 'care-full,' you find yourselves cared for."[4]

Care is so germane, so essential to a good conversation, that it often goes unnoticed. If you ask people to describe a list of ingredients that go into good communication, you'll find that care generally doesn't even make the list. But once you remove care from a conversation, your kids will notice immediately. When care is gone, the conversation is over. There is nothing left to discuss.

So if you want to talk so your kids will listen, you must be sure your heart is in the conversation. Why? Because if you don't really care, if you are distracted or disinterested, your kids won't care either.

> Quality time is when you and your child are together and keenly aware of each other. You are enjoying the same thing at the same time, even if it is just being in a room or going for a drive in the car.
>
> **Louise Lague**

That being said, you may be wondering what you can do, at a practical level, to cultivate a conversation that truly engages your child. Let us introduce you to a game that we know has worked wonders for many parents. It's called "verbal tennis," and it's easy to play.

You'll need two items: a tennis ball and a small notepad to use as a scorecard. If your children are young, you shouldn't have trouble convincing them to play this game with you. If you have teenagers, you might have a tougher sell, but it's worth it. To get their attention, you can tell them the game will improve the way they communicate with the opposite sex.

To start the game, sit a short distance apart from your child and ask an open-ended question. For example, "What can you tell me about your teacher?" As soon as you ask the question, toss the tennis ball to your child. She answers the question and then tosses the ball back to you. Then you can ask a follow-up question, such as, "Is she a tough teacher?" and toss the ball back.

Your child earns 10 points for every answered question; you can reward her with a prize of your choice when she receives 50 points. Once your child gets used to the game, reverse the roles and have her ask you questions. This is the real point of the game — to develop your child's ability to show interest and make a connection in a conversation.

Research plainly shows that people rate those who ask questions as far more interesting and as better communicators than those who talk only about themselves or don't talk at all. In short, we like people who ask us questions.

By the way, the next time you have adult friends over, encourage your child to practice verbal tennis with your guests. There's no need to throw a tennis ball, of course. The purpose of practicing with the ball is simply to give your child a mental image to use as she talks to others.

So give "verbal tennis" a shot. You may find it to be a fun and easy way to enjoy a conversation with your child that goes beyond those monosyllabic exchanges.

Connected Parents Maximize Quality Time

During morning quiet time with his two young daughters, Bill realized he hadn't been spending as much time with his girls as he wanted. After apologizing, he said, "You know, the quantity of time we spend together isn't always as important as the quality of time we spend together."

Kristen, six, and Madison, four, didn't quite understand.

Bill explained, "Quantity means how much time, and quality means how good the time is we spend together. Which would you rather have?"

Not missing a beat, Kristen replied, "Quality time—and a lot of it!"

Recent research backs up Kristin's point. The evidence clearly shows that children who spend time talking to their parents, taking part in family activities and meals, and building family traditions with their parents are less likely to engage in harmful activities. During these times of simply hanging out with their parents, kids tend to open up more easily about sensitive topics and explore issues in greater depth. Conversations about school, God, friends, and science projects rarely take place solely in a ten-minute chunk of "quality time" at the end of a long day.

So allow us to share a few practical ways to have a lot of quality time with your children. First, eat "slow food" together. It sounds simple, but when you're balancing work, a child's band practice, the cat's vet appointment, Little League, and church choir rehearsal, it can become routine to put the minivan on autopilot for the nearest drive-through. And that's too bad, because one of the best places to connect in meaningful conversation is around the dinner table—especially if you have teens. A study of 4,600 adolescents found that adolescents who ate more meals with their family suffered significantly lower rates of cigarette, alcohol, and drug abuse, enjoyed higher grade point averages, and struggled less with depression.[5] So if you don't do so already, make it a priority to sit down and eat a meal together as often as you can. Not only will you find the food to be more nourishing, but you'll be amazed at how the slower pace nourishes your family with good conversation.

Here's another idea. Take your child on a one-on-one vacation. I (Les) told you about the trip my dad and I took to follow the Oregon Trail. I have countless memories of those ten days—memories I hope to re-create in some fashion with my boys.

Our friends Sarah and Wil had long promised their children that when each child turned sixteen, he or she would go on an extended vacation with Mom or Dad; their daughter, Tina, would go with Mom, and their son, Ryan, with Dad. The only requirements were that the vacation had to take place in the continental United States and the kids had to help plan the trip.

"Money was tight, and we had to give up a lot in order to afford the vacations," Sarah explains, "but we knew how important it was to spend that time with each of the kids." Time alone with a parent during the teen years can be just the ticket for a teenager who needs to be reminded that she'll always have a safe place in her relationship with Mom and Dad as she moves out into the world.

Of course, the point is not the vacation. So if an extended holiday is impossible, try a long weekend with each of your children. And if a weekend away won't work, an overnighter at a local hotel or campground can go a long way toward strengthening the bond between you and your child.

The point is, if you are going to be a connected parent, you have to put in the time. Whether at mealtimes, after school over milk and cookies, during car rides, or at bedtime, connected parents build quality moments into the fast track of their daily lives.

For Discussion

1. On a scale of 1 to 10, how would you rank the importance of being a connected parent? Why?

2. On that same scale, how would you rank your natural inclination to build a bond with your child?

3. In specific terms, when are you most likely to feel connected with your child? Name the place or conditions. Would your child agree with you? How does your bonding manifest itself? (What do you say or do that conveys it?)

4. When is the next time you are likely to have an opportunity to connect with your child? What can you do now to maximize the opportunity?

CHAPTER 9

Commemorating Milestones: Are You a *Celebratory* Parent?

*Celebrate
what you want to see
more of.*
Tom Peters

We've spoken at hundreds of marriage seminars across the country, and one of the topics we almost always cover involves "unspoken rules." These are the deeply held expectations that a husband and wife bring into their marriage. They are unspoken because the husband and wife don't realize they have such rules until one spouse breaks them. And of all the unspoken rules we've heard about from couples over the years, the most common has to do with the celebration of birthdays and holidays. For example, the unspoken rule for one spouse might be, "A birthday should be planned and prepared for weeks in advance so the person feels thoroughly celebrated." Of course, this rule isn't articulated — at least not until the other spouse breaks the rule!

Some of us grew up in homes where birthdays were a very big deal preceded by much preparation and accompanied by much fanfare. Others of us grew up in homes where we were lucky to receive a card. Of course, when two people from these different camps marry, the sparks can fly — and we're not talking about the sparks from a birthday cake candle.

Whether you came from a home where celebrations were major events or minor mentions, we dedicate this chapter to helping you become a celebratory parent. Why? Because when we commemorate milestones with our kids, we are lavishing them with love in a powerful way that they will long remember.

Think about your most memorable birthday celebration. Remember your big present? You can probably even recall the decorations, the people who were there, and the feelings you had. Childhood celebrations are seared into our memories.

On my most memorable birthday, when I turned eight, I (Leslie) got to decorate my own chocolate cake. It was on a silver tray. But what I remember most is answering the door to find a birthday present I was longing for — a puppy.

Knowing the value of these kinds of celebrations, Les and I have worked hard to throw parties our boys will remember. Starting with John's first year, after months of many medical hurdles due to his premature birth, we threw a birthday party for him to which we invited one hundred people, including his surgeon, doctors and nurses, and other families we met in the neonatal intensive care unit (where John lived for his first three months), as well as family members from around the country and many local friends. Obviously, John doesn't remember a second of this special day, but he can review the photos and home video to see how we celebrated his first birthday.

> I can't believe it. Tomorrow there's absolutely nothing on my calendar. Let's celebrate.
>
> **Bess Truman**

Every celebratory parent knows the value of commemorating milestones. And even those parents who grew up in homes where celebrations were rare can learn to embrace a celebratory spirit.

The one who celebrates, according to the dictionary, "shows happiness that something good or special has happened." That definition hits the mark when it comes to being celebratory parents. These kinds of parents plan festivities to commemorate developmental milestones worth remembering.

Celebratus, the Latin origin of the English word *celebrate,* means "renowned" or "famous." It's where we get our word *celebrity.* And in a sense, that's what we do when we celebrate. We make famous—if only to our immediate family—a special happening or accomplishment.

By celebrating our kids' milestones, we are saying to them, "I notice you. I'm tuned in to your life, and I delight when something good or special happens to you." That's what celebrating means as a parent.

The Undeniable Importance of Being a Celebratory Parent

Every little life on this planet can be marked by milestones. The most celebrated, of course, are birthdays. Those are relatively easy. But many other milestones are worthy of celebrations. We have, of course, educational milestones, such as starting or completing a particular grade and ultimately graduating from high school or college. We also have spiritual milestones, such as a child's first communion or baptism. We have developmental milestones, such as sleeping in a "big boy" bed, learning to swim, getting a driver's license, or going on a first date. We have emotional milestones, such as moving past a

TEN TRAITS WORTH CONSIDERING

bad habit (biting one's nails) or responding more maturely to siblings. Every child's life is ripe with countless opportunities to celebrate.

Why should this matter? Because celebrations not only commemorate milestones worth remembering—they communicate a powerful message of love to a child. Linda Click of Adrian, Michigan, tells how for two months before her third birthday, her daughter Sandie said, "I'm going to have a party," countless times a day. When the great event was finally over, Sandie still told everyone, "I had a party." After several weeks, Linda and her husband grew weary of the repetition and finally told Sandie not to talk about the party anymore. For one whole day, Sandie didn't say a word about it. "But as I tucked her into bed that night," Linda explains, "Sandie prayed, 'Dear God, I had a birthday party.'"

Now there's one little girl who loves to be celebrated! But then, she isn't too different from any other child. Kids love celebrations because they are tangible reminders that they are loved.

In a survey of Americans' favorite activities during the Christmas season, cooking, baking, and eating ranked high. So did giving gifts and receiving gifts. But the top-ranked activity was "celebrating family traditions."[1] Conjure up your childhood Christmas traditions in your mind. Thinking about those traditions likely generates warm emotions that make you feel loved. Family celebrations almost always do—and that's the reason being a celebratory parent is so important.

> " 'Bring the fattened calf and kill it. Let's have a feast and celebrate. For this son of mine was dead and is alive again; he was lost and is found.' So they began to celebrate."
>
> **Luke 15:23**

A Self-Test: How Celebratory Are You?

The following true/false self-test is designed to get your wheels turning. Don't worry about trying to get the "right" answer; just give the answer that lines up with what you currently believe.

T   F   Being a celebratory parent means throwing great parties that outdo other parties your child has attended.

T   F   Celebrations for children should be relegated primarily to birthdays and graduations.

T   F   The primary message that stems from a celebration should be "see how much I did for you."

T   F   If you occasionally celebrate a child's accomplishments, he'll come to believe he's entitled to recognition and praise.

T   F   Being a celebratory parent is easy — requiring little effort or work.

Scoring: If you answered "true" to any of these five items, you will benefit from brushing up on how to be more celebratory with your child. Even if you answered "false" to each of these items, you can always learn new ways to become more celebratory.

How to Become a Celebratory Parent

Mike and his mother were in the doctor's office for his pre-school physical. The receptionist, completing his medical history, asked, "What is your birth date?"

"February 25," Mike answered.

"What year?" the receptionist asked.

"Every year," was Mike's matter-of-fact reply.

Good answer! In a child's mind, what matters is the celebration, not the historical data.

So if you're a parent who wants to cultivate this quality of marking your child's milestones with meaningful celebrations, what can you do? Allow us to share several practical tips.

> To show a child what has once delighted you, to find the child's delight added to your own, so that there is now a double delight seen in the glow of trust and affection, this is happiness.
>
> **J. B. Priestly**

Celebratory Parents Set Aside Their Tasks

I have to confess that if it weren't for Leslie, our family wouldn't celebrate nearly as often as we do. Why? Because I'm task oriented. I admit it. While Leslie is eager to stop and smell the proverbial roses, I'm charging forward to stay ahead of schedule. So when it comes to celebrating, I'm a little like the accomplished filmmaker Jerry Bruckheimer, who has said, "Well, I don't look back and celebrate. I just always worry about the next film."

I know just what he means. That's why I'm learning more and more how to make room in my hard-driving schedule for celebrations. In fact, even as we're writing this chapter, I'm realizing that I want my boys to remember me as a celebratory father. I want them to know their dad relished celebrating not only their accomplishments and their birthdays, but *them*!

Maybe this tendency to place a low priority on celebrating is a guy thing. I've talked with a few other dads about celebrating, and many of them feel the same way. I'm not saying it's necessarily a gender issue, but if you're like me and celebrating doesn't come easy, you need to learn to set aside your tasks and enjoy the ride.

Just recently I read a magazine interview with acclaimed Christian music artist Russ Taff. In it, he said this: "I was very much achievement-oriented my whole life. I was taught that as a child. 'So you have one Grammy Award, so what? You need another one.' I would never just sit down and enjoy. Since our baby came, however, I have learned to sit down—and enjoy!"[2]

Good for Russ! And good for all of us task-oriented parents who learn to enjoy the celebrations that mark the milestones of our children's lives.

> Rituals help us celebrate, and at the other end of the spectrum they help us to connect deeply with people in times of sorrow. The repetition that ritual always involves sets the present moment in a larger context and infuses it with wider meaning.
>
> **Huston Smith**

Celebratory Parents Maximize a Surprise

On her twelfth birthday, Alexa Ray was in New York City, and her pop musician father was in Los Angeles. He phoned her that morning to apologize for his absence and told her to expect the delivery of a large package before the end of the day. That evening Alexa answered the doorbell to find a brightly wrapped seven-foot-tall box. She tore it open, and out stepped her father, Billy Joel, fresh off the plane from the West Coast. Can you imagine her surprise?

Celebratory parents know how to milk a surprise. Our friend Linda recently told us about a surprise party that happened on her eighth birthday. Her mother planned a breakfast surprise party—but Linda was in on the surprise. Her mom sent out invitations to Linda's friends' parents, cautioning, "Shhhh, it's a surprise birthday party for Linda, but we don't want your daughter to know." The parents kept the party a secret, and then at 7:00 on Saturday morning, Linda's mom drove her minivan to each of the girls' homes. Linda, still in her pajamas, surprised them by waking them up. "Boy, were they surprised!" Linda says with a laugh, remembering the occasion as if it happened yesterday instead of some thirty years ago. "It was so fun to go and wake them up, and each friend I picked up before got to participate in waking the next girl. Then we all went to my house in our pajamas!"

Instead of a cake, Linda's mom made birthday pancakes. She set out banana slices, strawberries, blueberries, chocolate chips, and whipped cream so the girls could decorate their pancakes. The morning ended with the girls painting picture frames for a group picture to commemorate the surprise.

Sure, it takes some creative thought to be a celebratory parent, but it's well worth the effort. As Russian author Boris Pasternak said, "Surprise is the greatest gift which life can grant us." It's certainly a gift that celebratory parents understand.

> While we are living in the present, we must celebrate life every day, knowing that we are becoming history with every work, every action, every deed.
> **Mattie Stepanek**

Celebratory Parents Record Their Child's Experiences

Recently John and Jackson pulled their baby books off the shelf, without being prompted by Les or me, and started looking through them. They compared their thumbs to their baby footprints, and their hair to the locks of baby hair from their first haircuts. They laughed about the first words they ever uttered and delighted in reading the birthday cards that good friends had sent on their first birthdays.

I sometimes feel guilty that I don't have more of their first years recorded in these books, but I'm thrilled they love to review the details about their lives that I have managed to capture on these pages. The boys' excitement over their own biographies becomes even more evident when we play home movies and show photos on the television screen. Les is a bit of a photo junkie and has countless pictures of our two little guys. He has put many of them to music and burned them onto DVDs that our boys watch from time to time.

> The more you praise and celebrate your life, the more there is in life to celebrate.
>
> **Oprah Winfrey**

The point is, whenever parents record a piece of their child's life through a journal entry, a keepsake, a photo, or whatever, their child feels celebrated and loved. Not only that, but such tangible mementos serve to imbed the corresponding experiences in memory. "Almost anything you do today will be forgotten in just a few weeks," says research scientist John McCrone. "The ability to retrieve a memory decreases exponentially unless boosted by artificial aids such as diaries and photographs."[3]

By the way, if you have more than one child, you've probably already discovered the challenge of making sure your younger children receive as much attention as your firstborn. After all, when you experienced the exhilaration of having your first baby, your recording of his or her history may have bordered on obsession. "Every milestone of a firstborn is scrutinized, photographed, recorded, replayed, and retold by doting parents to admiring relatives and disinterested friends," says physician Marianne Neifert, "while subsequent children will strive to keep pace with the same adulation."[4] So take special care to record the experiences of the little ones who weren't your first.

Celebratory Parents Underscore Accomplishments

Grayson didn't have the easiest of years. His first grade experience involved moving to a new school after being bullied by a mean kid, getting help from tutors while other kids were enjoying recess, and putting forth a lot of extra effort. That's why his mom threw a big bash for his first grade class when the school year was over.

Julie, Grayson's mom, rented a local roller rink and invited all of his classmates for a couple of hours of memorable fun. Our son John is still talking about the occasion months later. "Remember when Mrs. Croutworst fell down while she was skating?" he asks, giggling. The event marked an accomplishment that was particularly important to Grayson—an accomplishment his mom wasn't about to let slide by without a bit of fanfare.

That's what celebratory parents do. While others may not see much of an achievement taking place, the parent who commemorates the triumph is saying, "I see you! You did it—and I'm proud of you!"

Most everyone celebrates a major graduation or the landing of a first job. But celebratory parents are on the lookout for other achievements to recognize. It may be learning how to swim or ride a bike. Perhaps it's passing a particularly tough class in high school. Or it may be reaching a personal goal, such as memorizing a passage of Scripture or saying kinder words to a sibling. The bottom line is that celebratory parents underscore a child's accomplishments when others may not even notice.

For Discussion

1. On a scale of 1 to 10, how would you rank the importance of being a celebratory parent? Why?

2. On that same scale, how would you rank your natural inclination to commemorate your child's milestones?

3. In specific terms, when are you most likely to celebrate your child—excluding birthdays and traditional holidays? Name the times or conditions. Would your child agree with you?

4. When is the next "nontraditional" occasion on which you are likely to celebrate your child? What can you do now to prepare for it?

CHAPTER 10

Keeping Your Word:
Are You an *Authentic* Parent?

*Live so that when your children
think of fairness and integrity,
they think of you.*

H. Jackson Brown

Recently our boys, John and Jackson, had been in bed for at least an hour when Leslie and I returned from a dinner out with friends. We debriefed with the babysitter and then sneaked into the boys' room to kiss them good-night.

"Dad, can I have some ice cream?" Jackson whispered.

"No, Jack, it's late, way past bedtime."

"But, Daddy, you promised you'd get ice cream while you were gone."

He was right. Jack had asked for ice cream earlier in the day, but we didn't have any. So I told him, "If you eat up all your green beans, I'll get some for you while I'm out—I promise."

> No legacy is so rich as honesty.
>
> **William Shakespeare**

Dinner came and went. We cleaned up the kitchen; the boys picked up their toys. The sitter arrived. And Leslie and I left for our evening with friends.

I'd forgotten all about the ice cream. But Jackson hadn't.

So even though it was after ten o'clock, I hopped in the car, drove to the grocery store, bought a pint of cookies and cream, and hurried home. Jack and I enjoyed a late-night bowl together. Why? Because I promised. And I want my sons to grow up trusting their daddy's word. I want them to know that I can be counted on—that I'm sincere, genuine, and trustworthy.

Of course, following through on a promise to get ice cream is small potatoes compared to what is sometimes required of a parent to be authentic. Consider Michael Jordan, indisputably the leading player in the NBA for over a decade. Interestingly, he was never the highest-paid player. When asked why he didn't do what so many other players do—hold out on their contracts until they get more money—Michael replied, "I have always honored my word. I went for security. I had six-year contracts, and I always honored them. People said I was underpaid, but when I signed on the dotted line, I gave my word."[1]

> We must have infinite faith in each other.
>
> **Henry David Thoreau**

Three years later, after several highly visible players reneged on their contracts, a reporter asked Michael once again about being underpaid, and he explained that if his kids saw their dad breaking a promise, he couldn't rightly continue training them to keep their word. By not asking for a contract renegotiation, Michael Jordan spoke volumes to his children. He told them, "You stand by your word, even when that might go against you."

Do you think his kids will remember that message? Of course! They saw him live it out. He didn't just preach the message; he walked his talk. He was authentic—the real deal. And being authentic isn't always easy as a parent.

AUTHENTIC AUTHENTIC AUTH
ENTIC AUTHENTIC AUTHENTIC
HENTIC AUTHENTIC AUTHEN

Look up the word *authentic*, and you'll find a variety of synonyms: bona fide, genuine, real, sincere, true, unquestionable. But you'll also find a phrase that appears under this word in nearly every dictionary: "worthy of trust." This phrase cuts to the heart of what it means to be an authentic parent. *Authentic* derives from the Greek *anyein*, which means "to accomplish." And any parent who has become worthy of trust in the eyes of a son or daughter—especially as the child matures—has accomplished a great deal.

Modeling integrity consistently and staying true to your word are no small feats. But this kind of conduct is what authenticity as a parent demands. In simplest terms, authentic parents have succeeded in being genuine while at the same time maintaining their child's trust and respect. And when you are genuine, when you are true to your convictions, you run the risk of rejection at the deepest and most vulnerable level. Every parent of a prodigal can attest to the pain that this kind of rejection provokes.

Are we saying that being genuine increases your chances of eventual rejection? Far from it! Every time you keep your word as a parent, you show your child just how trustworthy you are.

The Undeniable Importance of Being an Authentic Parent

A child who continually questions her parent's authenticity, who wonders time and again whether her mom or dad is being truthful, for example, will forever struggle with "trust issues." Ask any psychologist and you'll get the same response: Without the solid foundation of an authentic and trustworthy relationship at home, a child will become an adult who carries deep suspicions not only of authority figures but of everyone else as well.

If the mistrust is deep enough, a parent can unwittingly rob a child of her capacity to make friends and find love. "We're never so vulnerable than when we trust someone," said American painter Walter Anderson, "but paradoxically, if we cannot trust, neither can we find love." True love is predicated upon the capacity to trust.

Even if a person is trustworthy, a truly suspicious child won't find him to be so. That's what Thoreau was getting at when he said, "We are always paid for our suspicion by finding what we suspect." In other words, if you are unintentionally raised to be on the lookout for ways that people are unreliable, untruthful, and conniving, that's exactly what you'll find.

> When two people relate to each other authentically and humanly, God is the electricity that surges between them.
>
> **Martin Buber**

The bottom line is that every child needs an authentic parent who is deserving of her trust. Why? Because this bedrock quality opens a child's spirit to loving relationships. "Oh, the comfort, the inexpressible comfort of feeling safe with a person," wrote George Eliot, "having neither to weigh thoughts nor to measure words, but pouring them all out, just as they are, chaff and grain together, certain that a faithful hand will take and sift them, keep what is worth keeping, and with a breath of kindness blow the rest away." The writer may not have been talking specifically about a parent-child relationship when they penned these words, but the sentiments certainly fit. A child will pour out what she is truly feeling and thinking only in the comfortable presence of a trustworthy person.

In the absence of an authentic parent, a child's capacity for the fundamentals of faith, hope, and love will hardly have a fighting chance. When a child is without a trustworthy parent, faith in others (and ultimately in God) is weakened. Hope for the future is diminished. And love becomes elusive. So we'll say it once more: It's difficult to exaggerate the importance of being an authentic parent.

A Self-Test: How Authentic Are You?

The following true/false self-test is designed to get your wheels turning. Don't worry about trying to get the "right" answer; just give the answer that lines up with what you currently believe.

   T   F   More important than who I am is who my child thinks I am.

   T   F   "Do what I say and not what I do" is a motto every parent should live by.

   T   F   I'm automatically trustworthy to my child by virtue of being his parent.

   T   F   Respecting a teenager means giving him unquestionable freedom.

   T   F   I can't trust my child if he doesn't give me reliable evidence to help me trust him.

Scoring: If you answered "true" to any of these five items, you will benefit from brushing up on how to be more authentic with your child. Even if you answered "false" to each of these items, you can always learn new ways to become more authentic.

How to Become an Authentic Parent

Many products are designed to imitate the real thing. You can buy plastic decking that looks like real wood, or vinyl flooring that appears to be ceramic tile. You can buy fake fur, fake jewelry, and fake hairpieces. The purpose behind all of these items is to present an image that looks as real as possible — but isn't.

Recently we even heard about a product called Sprayonmud, designed for use on the outside of your SUV. That way you can fool others into thinking that you use your expensive gas-guzzler for more than taking the kids to soccer practice. Spray it on and friends might think you've just returned from a wilderness adventure. You may think we're joking, but it's a real product, developed in London, and sells for about $15 a bottle. And it's one of the best examples we've seen of just how willing some people are to be phony.

> The most exhausting thing you can do is to be inauthentic.
>
> **Anne Morrow Lindbergh**

The same holds true for most parents. We can, at times, present an image that isn't authentic. We may make a promise but never follow through. We may preach a message we want our kids to follow even though we don't follow it ourselves. Nearly every parent has struggled with being the real deal on occasion. Here are just a few of the ways we try to pass off something fake for the genuine article:

- We may punish our child for acting out when we can't seem to keep a lid on our own anger.
- We may assure our child we won't embarrass her by talking about her retainer in front of her friends — and then do just that.
- We may pretend something will be easy when, in actuality, it will be quite difficult.

- We may talk about how important it is to be kind and then, when we think our child isn't listening, say something rude behind someone's back.
- We may promise to keep a secret and then blab it to our child's teacher or another parent.

Authenticity comes down to being worthy of your child's trust. And if this is your goal, you can't "spray on" platitudes to cover what he knows isn't real. The only way to garner your child's trust is to prove, through a multitude of experiences, that you are trustworthy. Consider the father who is playing with his little boy, throwing him in the air and catching him just before he hits the ground. The child is having a great time, saying, "Do it again! Do it again!" Rather than being stiff with fear, he's nimble and trusting. How can he be so carefree and happy? Because he has a history with his daddy. He has played this game dozens of times and his dad has never dropped him. He's confident and relaxed because he trusts his dad to catch him.

A friend of ours who works in the science department at our university often says, "Parenthood requires constant proofs." What he means is that a child needs to be shown, through experience, the evidence that his parents are worthy of trust—just like the child whose dad throws him into the air and catches him. The best way to cultivate this kind of trust? By remembering that authentic parents are trustworthy when they "walk their talk" and when they trust their children. Let's take a look at each.

Authentic Parents Are Trustworthy When They Walk Their Talk

Julian Lennon was abandoned by his father, Beatle John Lennon, at age five. Any child who has experienced such a profound betrayal by a father will invariably lose respect, regardless of Dad's accomplishments, and almost always grow bitter. Julian is no exception. When asked if he could respect his father all these years later, even after his father's death, Julian replied, "He was a hypocrite. Dad could talk about peace and love out loud to the world, but he could never show it to the people who supposedly meant the most to him: his wife and son. How can you talk about peace and love and have a family in bits and pieces—no communication, adultery, and divorce? You can't do it, not if you're being true and honest with yourself."[2]

Who can disagree? A child who doesn't see congruence in what a parent preaches and what a parent does is bound to see that parent as a phony. And let's be honest, we all can be hypocrites at times. We can talk a good talk—especially to our children. But they'll eventually see right through it if we don't back it up with our walk.

Robert Weygand, a Rhode Island landscaper, is a great example of a parent who walks his talk. He had just finished a $34,000 proposal to do work in Pawtucket's Slater Memorial Park when the mayor called. "I want you to bump up the contract by five—three thousand dollars for me and two thousand dollars for you."

Weygand was shocked by the mayor's blatant bid rigging and didn't know what to do. If he refused the mayor, he knew he would never get another city job. Plus, even if he went public, he didn't know if people would believe him. Besides, his company desperately needed this contract just to make payroll.

> Level with your child by being honest. Nobody spots a phony quicker than a child.
>
> **Mary MacCracken**

But just when he'd convinced himself that he had no options, three pictures came to his mind—his three children, Jennifer, Allison, and Bobby. What would they think of their dad if it came out that he had taken a bribe to get government work?

So here's what Weygand did: He called the state police, who called the FBI, and a few weeks later, Weygand returned to city hall carrying a white envelope filled with $1,250. He also brought one more item — a discreet tape recorder. And when the mayor asked about the rest of his money, FBI agents were waiting to arrest him. They had all the evidence they needed.[3]

After the story hit the press, Weygand received numerous threatening phone calls for bringing down the mayor, but that didn't matter at home. Jennifer, Allison, and Bobby saw their dad as a hero — a man who held to his convictions in spite of strong temptations.

Of course, a parent doesn't need to "walk his talk" in such a dramatic way to earn the trust and respect of his children. As parents, we earn more trust every time we keep our word, fulfill a promise, live by our own rules, and practice what we preach.

Authentic Parents Are Trustworthy When They Trust Their Children

A mountain of material has been produced for teaching children to respect their parents. But you'll have to look a bit harder to find information on how parents can respect their children. Strange, too, since respecting our kids is vital to becoming trustworthy parents.

"Trust men and they will be true to you," said Ralph Waldo Emerson, "treat them greatly and they will show themselves great." The same holds true for kids. In fact, the surest way to garner your child's trust and respect is to show your child that you genuinely trust and respect her. This simple act, more than anything else you do as a parent, will engender a mutual authenticity that roots your relationship in love and allows your child to see just how trustworthy you are.

Here are some of the most common ways to show your child respect:

- Make eye contact when your child is talking to you.
- Knock before entering your child's room, especially if the door is closed.

- Value your child's need for fun and the time he spends with his friends.
- Give your child space to have different opinions and preferences than you (or other members of the family).
- Value your child's need for privacy. Don't open her mail or listen in on her phone conversations.
- If your child is struggling with something and is in no danger of getting hurt, hurting someone else, or ruining something valuable, ask him if he wants help before you step in and do something for him.
- When someone asks your child a question, let your child answer for himself. Resist the temptation to speak for your child, especially when he is present.

We can show respect on many levels. I (Leslie) always want to rush in to settle a tiff between our two boys. Les takes a different approach. He gives them time to work it out on their own. He listens quietly from the next room to see what they do without intervention. And I have to admit that some of the sweetest moments we ever hear in our house occur when the two of them apologize without being prodded. At their young ages, they probably have no idea what we are doing in these instances, but we do. Allowing them to resolve conflict on their own is a way we show them respect.

Of course, as children grow older, the issue becomes dicier. Why? Because most teens make the mistake of equating respect with permission. "If you respect me, you'll let me ..." But that's not true! Respect and permission are two different things. You can respect your children without allowing them to do whatever they want. In fact, if you do this properly, you will become all the more trustworthy in their eyes. The key is to listen completely to them before drawing conclusions or making decisions. Take this extra time. It may or may not change your mind, but listen first.

You also might want to take a good look at your rules. As children mature, rules need to be revised. You want your rules to be logical, fair, reasonable, and truthful. Often parents make rules out of convenience for themselves. Sometimes they make rules to assuage their fears or satisfy their need for control. Resist such temptation by talking to your child about why you have certain rules.

> My daughters have taught me that I don't have to be God; I just need to be real.
> **Gloria Gaither**

Finally, when your child disappoints you, make a distinction between his behavior and his character. It's one thing to point out wrong actions, but be careful not to attack your child's character in the process.

As you do these things consistently, you'll be showing your kids trust and respect—even though you don't always agree to their requests. This balance of guidance and trust is a valuable example of how your kids can extend respect to you—even when you don't see eye to eye.

To sum it up, authentic parents are worthy of trust because they are exactly what they claim to be. They're not creating an image or pretending to be something they're not. And they're not copying other parents who seem to have already won the respect of their children. Authentic parents are comfortable in their own skin and deserving of their children's trust.

For Discussion

1. On a scale of 1 to 10, how would you rank the importance of being an authentic parent? Why?

2. On that same scale, how would you rank your natural inclination to keep your word with your child?

3. In specific terms, when are you most likely to demonstrate authenticity with your child? Name the place or conditions. Would your child agree with you?

4. When is the next time you are likely to have an opportunity to demonstrate authenticity with your child? What can you do now to maximize the opportunity?

CHAPTER 11

Creating the Safest Place on Earth: Are You a *Comforting* Parent?

Love is, above all, the gift of oneself.
Jean Anouilh

John Trent, a fellow psychologist and good friend of ours, is well known for writing many helpful books. But of all the books he has authored, the one that is talked about most in our home is a children's book titled *I'd Choose You*. Our boys love the story of the little elephant named Norbert. The pachyderm's day begins badly but improves significantly when his parents tell him that out of all the kids in the world—including the flamingo who's a champion ice-skater, the rhino who's not afraid to jump off the high dive, and even the caterpillar who will grow to be a butterfly one day—they chose him.

This little book took on particular meaning to us when John told us the story of Danny, a boy who had an especially strong affinity for this story. When Danny was six years old, his parents were far away at a medical conference. Simultaneously each of their beepers went off. It was an emergency page from the couple who were watching him. Danny was running a high fever and they needed instructions. The parents immediately called a pediatrician friend who made some suggestions and called in a prescription. But the boy's fever shot up so high and so quickly that they rushed him to a local hospital. Doctors were finally able to bring Danny's temperature down and save his life, but the fever robbed him of his hearing in both ears.

After the fever took little Danny's hearing, it became obvious that his parents would need a way other than spoken words to communicate their love and commitment to him. So the three of them learned sign language together. The first words they asked the speech pathologist to teach them? *I'd choose you.*

> To ease another's heartache is to forget one's own.
>
> **Abraham Lincoln**

"We wanted him to hear those words again from us," the parents told John.

With a child who had suffered through multiple surgeries ourselves, we identified deeply with this couple as John told us their story. In fact, we all had eyes rimmed with tears as he recounted it. For what else is a parent good for if not the comfort of letting a little one know that he is chosen, imperfections and all, by a mom and dad who love him deeply? This message creates the safest place on earth for a child, and the comfort it affords will stay with a child forever.

COMFORTING

Chicken noodle soup, meat loaf, fried chicken, macaroni and cheese, mashed potatoes and gravy, bread pudding, brownies, donuts, apple pie. These are commonly referred to as "comfort food." And with good reason. Most of us find great comfort in a tasty meal we've grown up with, a meal that doesn't have to be explained by *Gourmet Magazine* or *Saveur*.

But true comfort, the kind that heals emotional hurts and turns around bad days, involves far more than our palate. The dictionary defines it as a feeling of pleasurable ease, well-being, and contentment. But a quick review of the word's origin uncovers a deeper meaning. We get the word *comfort* from the Latin *com* + *fortis*, meaning "to make strong" (like a fortress).

So to comfort literally means to make someone stronger. And that's exactly what a parent does for a child. Comfort fortifies a child's spirit. Whenever we encourage a child with uplifting words, console her with a tender touch, relieve her sorrow with our mere presence, or support her with heartfelt praise, we make that child strong.

The Undeniable Importance of Being a Comforting Parent

When a child rests in the safety of a parent's comfort, his confidence and courage expand. A parent's comfort gives a child strength to venture out and grow. It provides the security he needs to move beyond his current comfort zone.

Several months ago our family was having fun at a hotel swimming pool in Vancouver, British Columbia. I (Les) was swimming in the deep end by the diving board when my three-year-old, Jackson, came tottering down the steps into the shallow end of the pool. He can't swim yet, but he wears big blue "floaties" around each arm. He can't sink with his floaties on.

> Words of comfort, skillfully administered, are the oldest therapy known to man.
>
> **Louis Nizer**

As soon as Jackson moved away from the steps, he called to me, "Daddy, I'm scared. I want to come where you are."

"Jackson, it's a lot deeper down here," I told him.

"I don't care. I want to be where you are," he replied.

"Okay, come on," I said, treading water with my head just above the surface.

He began dog-paddling across the pool, splashing past the three-foot-deep ... six-foot-deep ... ten-foot-deep markers. When he came up to me, he grabbed my neck, his look of panic giving way to relief. Next to his father, he felt secure, and the depth or the danger of the water made very little difference.

> To feel that one has a place in life solves half the problems of contentment.
>
> **George Woodberry**

That's exactly what the comfort of a parent provides: security. And without emotional security, a child will sink like a stone. Emotional security is the foundation of a fulfilling and productive life. It is the key ingredient in self-esteem and self-reliance, and it is the platform for academic performance, friendship, family bonds, and solid core values. In short, it's what makes a child strong.

Even in a "normal" home, emotional security is not a given for children. More than forty years of research in developmental psychology laboratories around the world have shown that 20 to 30 percent of children develop some form of insecure connection with their parents.[1] These are children from two-parent, middle-income families! Insecurity, it seems, comes part and parcel with growing up.

The point is that even loving parents can't take this trait for granted. The comfort provided by emotional security deserves the attention of every parent.

A Self-Test: How Comforting Are You?

The following true/false self-test is designed to get your wheels turning. Don't worry about trying to get the "right" answer; just give the answer that lines up with what you currently believe.

T F   The fact that a child wants to be close to you automatically means she is strongly attached to you.

T F   One of the best ways to comfort a disgruntled child is to solve his problem for him.

T F   If you comfort a child too much, you run the risk of raising a child with no backbone.

T F   Physical touch is a relatively unreliable way of conveying comfort.

T F   If the parent doesn't talk about it, a child rarely picks up on his parent's anxiety.

Scoring: If you answered "true" to any of these five items, you will benefit from brushing up on how to be more comforting to your child. Even if you answered "false" to each of these items, you can always learn new ways to become more comforting.

How to Become a Comforting Parent

About a month ago, our friend Steve bought his two-year-old daughter, Sarah, an aquarium. They went together to the pet store to pick out four fish to put in the tank. Two weeks later, Sarah found one of the fish dead. It was caught up in one of the fake plastic plants. Sarah, in her two-year-old way, explained to her dad that the fish had died in the "bushes."

"I realized that this was the first of many losses she would experience in life," Steve told us. "I broke into tears, however, when she said to me, 'Daddy, keep me from getting caught in the bushes.'"

Every child, no matter what age or stage, looks to her parents for comfort. Children rely on Mom and Dad to keep them out of the bushes. And while we can't always protect them from harm, we can provide great comfort. Let's explore some of the most effective ways to create the safest place on earth for our kids.

Comforting Parents Give Warm Embraces

The deadliest earthquake in the last ten years filled the nation of Iran with sadness. But in the midst of despair, one story gave people hope. Cradled in her dead mother's arms, surrounded by the crumbled remnant of a collapsed building, a baby girl was found alive.

Six-month-old Nassim's mother protected her from the falling wreckage to save her life. Rescuers found the girl thirty-seven hours after the earthquake. Hessamoddin Farrokhyar, Red Crescent public relations deputy director in Tehran, said, "She is alive because of her mother's embrace."[2]

Hugging our children is a protective instinct. What parent would not have done the same as this terrified mother? But this instinct is something most parents take for granted. In fact, as loving parents, we hug our children without much thought, never realizing just how much our embrace can build up their emotional security. "Skin cells offer a direct path into the deep reservoir of emotion we metaphorically call the human heart," said Dr. Paul Brand. And anthropologist Helen Fisher, in her book *Anatomy of Love*, describes the importance of touch this way: "Human skin is like a field of grass, each blade a nerve ending so sensitive that the slightest graze can etch into the human brain a memory of the moment."[3]

> When we determine to be there for our children, the moment arrives one day when we discover they love to be there for us.
>
> **John Trent**

Baby Nassim will carry the value of her mother's embrace all her days. And so will your children — regardless of their age. It doesn't take the tragedy of an earthquake to share the comfort of a warm embrace that will be remembered forever.

Comforting Parents Are Intentional about Including Their Children

My dad was a college president, and because of his busy life, I (Les) often tagged along to events and dinners where no other kids were present — especially after my two older brothers were no longer living at home. Now, that might sound like a drag, and sometimes it was. But Mom and Dad always went out of their way to be sure I was included. If they were meeting others for dinner, they'd be sure I made meaningful connections with other adults at the table. They'd pull me into conversations and highlight topics they knew would interest me. They'd even ask for my advice. Of course, they could have carried on as though I wasn't really supposed to be there, but they didn't. They included me. And that always gave me comfort.

It's true for every child. When a parent includes a child in any activity — whether it be cooking, working in the garage, or washing the car, the child is sure to enjoy the pleasurable comfort of being loved.

A freelance reporter for the *New York Times* once interviewed Marilyn Monroe. She was aware of Marilyn's past and the fact that during her early years Marilyn had been shuffled from one foster home to another. The reporter asked, "Did you ever feel loved by any of the foster families with whom you lived?"

"Once," Marilyn replied, "when I was about seven or eight. The woman I was living with was putting on makeup, and I was watching her. She was in a happy mood, so she reached over and patted my cheeks with her rouge puff.... For that moment, I felt loved by her."

It doesn't take much to include a child in the humdrum of life. And when you do, you're sure to ease her spirit and build her confidence with comfort.

Comforting Parents Exhibit
a Non-Anxious Presence

One night a child was late coming home for supper; when her worried father met her at the door, she explained that on her way she had encountered a friend who had broken her favorite doll on the sidewalk.

"So you stopped to help her pick up the pieces?" her father asked.

"Oh no," she answered. "I stopped and helped her cry."

Like this child, every parent has the ability to be a non-anxious presence by simply being with a child while she cries. But exhibiting a non-anxious presence can be a tall order for some parents. After all, most of us have plenty to be anxious about and feel that we need to say or do the right thing in the right way. But such anxiety is typically self-defeating. It compels us to blurt out answers to questions our children aren't asking. We get wound up with words to alleviate hurt feelings or disappointments when all our children need is to know we are standing nearby when they are ready to talk.

Think of a non-anxious presence as a state of inner calm. You are connected to your child but are levelheaded when it comes to their swirling emotions. Of course, being levelheaded doesn't mean stuffing your feelings; it means remaining objective. A non-anxious presence is particularly valuable in conflict. The capacity to remain calm during conflict may be one of your most significant capabilities as a

> A rich emotional connection with our children is the best legacy we can leave them and the finest inheritance they can have.
>
> **Zeynep Biringen**

parent. Not only can it enable you to be more adroit in difficult situations, but it can lessen anxiety throughout your entire family — because it brings comfort. Sometimes this attribute can do more to resolve tense issues than the ability to come up with good solutions.

Comforting Parents See
What Others Don't See

We opened this chapter by telling you about the children's book *I'd Choose You.* These three words, perhaps more than any others, can give profound comfort to a child's heart. Why? Because they convey the idea, "Mom and Dad love me even if I'm unlovely." When a toddler snaps, "I hate you," for example, comforting parents hear words that others don't. They hear "I'm scared," or "I got my feelings hurt." So they continue to "choose" the child because they see and hear what others don't.

We don't know of a parent who lives out the "I'd choose you" sentiment any more powerfully than Joyce Daugherty, a member of Southeast Christian Church in Louisville, Kentucky. Not long ago, she traveled to an orphanage in Donetsk, Ukraine, and it was there that she saw two-year-old Kristen. Her beautiful blue eyes framed the edges of a facial tumor, a hemangioma, but even that could not hide Kristen's impish grin.

"Kristen's eyes were so alert that I just kept watching her," says Daugherty. "There was something special that tumor could not hide. I could have taken any of the children I saw home with me. At the same time, I knew if I adopted Kristen, she'd have more than a new start — she'd have a new life."

"These children are throw-aways in Ukraine," says Nancy Stanbery, who has helped facilitate more than 130 adoptions in Ukraine. "Most Ukrainian families are afraid of a child with any kind of disability. Mothers take them to an orphanage or abandon them in a public place, walk away and never look back."[4]

Daugherty chose Kristen. Last year, a Louisville surgeon removed the hemangioma. Thin scars are healing and everything about Kristen has changed dramatically. She chatters constantly, saying, "I love you," over and over again to her momma.

Every time you look past words or actions or even appearances that aren't lovely—and love a child anyway—you're saying, "I choose you." And remember, you're doing more than soothing your child's spirit. You're building a fortress of love, the safest place on earth, around her heart.

> Even though I walk through the valley
> of the shadow of death, I will fear no evil,
> for you are with me; your rod and your staff,
> they comfort me.
>
> **Psalm 23:4**

For Discussion

1. On a scale of 1 to 10, how would you rank the importance of being a comforting parent? Why?

2. On that same scale, how would you rank your natural inclination to create the safest place on earth for your child?

3. In specific terms, when are you most likely to demonstrate the acts of comfort outlined in this chapter (such as including your child, exhibiting a non-anxious presence, and so on)?

4. When is the next time you are likely to have an opportunity to demonstrate an act of comfort with your child? What can you do now to maximize the opportunity?

CHAPTER 12

Instilling Wisdom:
Are You an *Insightful* Parent?

*A moment's insight is sometimes worth
a lifetime's experience.*
Oliver Wendell Holmes

Benjamin, eight years old, enters the bedroom of his mother, who is dying of cancer. He is excited as she gives him his Christmas present —a magician's cape with photographs of the two of them embedded on it. Benjamin sits in front of her and asks, "Are you dying?"

His mother pauses for a moment, then asks, "What do you think?"

Sadly he answers, "Yes. I won't see you anymore."

She tells him, "Well, you won't see my body, but ... you know how a caterpillar becomes something else?"

Benjamin nods. "A butterfly."

She continues, "Yeah, you just have to think of me as off flying somewhere. And of course, a magician knows the secret that just because you don't see something, it doesn't mean it's not there." She makes a coin appear from his ear, and they both laugh.

Benjamin asks her where she'll be. She takes his hand, kisses it, places it in front of his heart, and says, "Right here. Inside the magician."

"Can I talk to you when you're there?"

"Always. Always. Always. You won't hear my voice, but deep inside, you'll know what I'm saying."

"It's not good enough."

"No, no, of course it isn't, because it isn't everything. And we want everything, don't we? But we still have one thing. One of the greatest things we will always have. Do you know what that is? Our dreams."

Benjamin gives a small smile.

"We can still meet in our dreams," his mother continues. "We can talk to each other there, go for walks together in the summer, and in the winter and in the rain and in the sun. I can come and pick you up and we can go flying."

Starting to get teary-eyed, he says, "Nobody loves you more than me."

He gives her a big hug as she says, "Nobody ever will."[1]

It's a poignant scene from the movie *Stepmom*, starring Susan Sarandon. And it beautifully portrays the finesse of a wise and insightful parent. She's astute, sensitive, and intuitive — qualities that aren't always common in parenthood. But not because wisdom is the exclusive domain of bearded old sages. That's a mere caricature. "It is not white hair that engenders wisdom," said Greek dramatist Menander. And Titus Maccius Plautus said, "Not by age but by capacity is wisdom acquired." Wisdom can be caught and taught. It can be honed. That's why Proverbs urges us to get wisdom at all costs.[2] And that's exactly what the insightful parent does.

> To acquire knowledge, one must study; but to acquire wisdom, one must observe.
>
> **Marilyn vos Savant**

INSIGHTFUL INSIGHTFUL INSIGHTFUL INSIGHTFUL INSIGHTFUL INSIGHTFUL INSIGHTFUL INSIGHTFUL INSIGHTFUL INSIGHTFUL INSIGHT

The English preacher Charles Spurgeon said, "Wisdom is the right use of knowledge. To know is not to be wise." He's right. If you look up either *wisdom* or *insight* in the dictionary, you won't find even a mention of knowledge. Yet that's a common misperception — that a wise person is filled with knowledge. More accurately, it's what a person does with his knowledge that makes him insightful or wise. In fact, that's just what Spurgeon went on to say: "To know how to use knowledge is to have wisdom."

The dictionary says that those with insight have "penetrating understanding." They have a clear and deep perception of people and circumstances. They grasp the inward or hidden nature of things. And so, an insightful parent is perceptive, thoughtful, sensitive, and intuitive. An insightful parent instills wisdom.

The Undeniable Importance of Being an Insightful Parent

In our personal library at home, we have dozens of parenting books. They line several shelves. Some have been given to us, while others were purchased for specific reasons and have been studied with great intention. Even more were required by professors of several graduate classes we took years ago. It's fair to say that we have studied parenting for more than two decades from several different angles. But all this study does very little to ensure that we are becoming insightful parents. It doesn't guarantee we'll put our knowledge to use by making wise decisions.

Good parenting requires more than intellect. It touches a dimension of the personality that's too often ignored, in part because having insight is not always easy to describe. Wisdom is abstract. The quality of being affirming or comforting conjures up immediate mental images. Insight is more ambiguous. So does it really matter whether our kids have insightful parents? You bet!

Not far from our home in Seattle is a world-renowned center for research on parent-child interactions. The center is directed by Dr. John Gottman at the University of Washington. He and his team have conducted in-depth research into 119 families, observing how parents and children relate to one another. He has been following these children from age four to adolescence. His studies involve lengthy interviews with parents, talking about their marriages, their reactions to their children's emotional experiences, and their own awareness of their role in their children's lives. He has checked in with these families over time to see how the children are developing in terms of health, academic achievement, emotional development, and social relationships.

His results tell a simple yet compelling story. He has found that most parents fall into one of two broad categories: those who give their children guidance about the world of emotion and those who don't. He calls the parents who get involved with their children's feelings "Emotion Coaches." You might say that these parents practice "penetrating understanding." Much like athletic coaches, they study their children and teach them how to deal with life. They don't object to their children's displays of anger, sadness, or fear. Nor do they ignore them. Instead, they accept negative emotions as a fact of life and use emotional moments as opportunities to teach their kids important life lessons.

What difference does it make when children have insightful parents? By observing and analyzing in detail the words, actions, and emotional responses of families over time, Dr. Gottman has discovered a truly significant contrast. Children whose parents consistently practice Emotion Coaching have better physical health and score higher academically than children whose parents don't offer such guidance. These kids get along better with friends, have fewer behavioral problems, and are less prone to acts of violence. Overall, children who are Emotion Coached experience fewer negative feelings and more positive feelings. In short, they're healthier mentally, physically, and spiritually.[3]

But the result that has surprised Dr. Gottman most is this: When mothers and fathers work to intentionally instill wisdom through Emotion Coaching, their children become more resilient. They are better able to soothe themselves, bounce back from distress, and carry on with productive activities. In other words, they are more emotionally intelligent.

A Self-Test: How Insightful Are You?

The following true/false self-test is designed to get your wheels turning. Don't worry about trying to get the "right" answer; just give the answer that lines up with what you currently believe.

T   F   Part of being a wise parent is to always be honest and forthright with anything a child wants to know.

T   F   An insightful parent will help a child avoid as many struggles and mistakes as possible.

T   F   Helping a child manage urges and impulses is next to impossible.

T   F   The insightful parent almost always has an answer for nearly anything a child might want to know.

T   F   You should never let your child see your mistakes.

Scoring: If you answered "true" to any of these five items, you will benefit from brushing up on how to be more insightful with your child. Even if you answered "false" to each of these items, you can always learn new ways to become more insightful.

How to Become an Insightful Parent

"Most of what I really need to know about how to live, and what to do, and how to be, I learned in kindergarten." So writes Robert Fulghum in his wildly popular book *All I Really Need to Know I Learned in Kindergarten.* "Wisdom," he says, "was not at the top of the graduate school mountain, but there in the sandbox at nursery school."[4]

What did he learn in the sandbox? Share everything. Play fair. Don't hit people. Put things back where you found them. Clean up your own mess. Don't take things that aren't yours. Say you're sorry when you hurt somebody. Hold hands. Stick together.

Let's face it, children are often wiser than we know. Perhaps that's part of what Jesus was getting at when he said, "Unless you change and become like little children, you will never enter the kingdom of heaven."[5]

So why is being a wise and insightful parent such a challenge? Maybe it's because we put so much emphasis on knowledge in our parenting that wisdom gets pushed to the side. Whatever the reason, we want to pass along some insights that will help you become, well, more insightful.

> A child's hand in yours — what tenderness it arouses, what power it conjures. You are instantly the very touchstone of wisdom and strength.
> **Marjorie Holmes**

Insightful Parents Are Discerning

In her book *The Hiding Place*, Corrie ten Boom tells of an event that took place when she was eleven or twelve years old as she traveled with her father on a train from Amsterdam to Haarlem. She had stumbled upon a poem with the phrase "sex sin" among its lines, and so, seated next to her father in the train compartment, she innocently asked, "Father, what is sex sin?"

> He turned to look at me, as he always did when answering a question, but, to my surprise, he said nothing. At last he stood up, lifted his traveling case from the rack over our heads, and set it on the floor.
>
> "Will you carry it off the train, Corrie?" he asked.
>
> I stood up and tugged at it. It was crammed with watches and spare parts he had purchased that morning.
>
> "It's too heavy," I said.
>
> "Yes," he said. "And it would be a pretty poor father who would ask his little girl to carry such a load. It's the same way, Corrie, with knowledge. Some knowledge is too heavy for children. When you are older and stronger, you can bear it. For now you must trust me to carry it for you."[6]

Corrie, as a young girl, was satisfied. "More than satisfied," she writes, "wonderfully at peace. There were answers to this and all my hard questions; for now, I was content to leave them in my father's keeping."

Every insightful parent can identify with Corrie's father. After all, wisdom is found in knowing what not to share. It has a judicious and discriminating quality that protects a child from knowledge that is too heavy. Of course, Hollywood has made an attempt to help parents discriminate between movies by using a rating system, but wise parents know that far more discernment is needed in a child's life than that. A child may need to be protected, for example, from a particular conversation (such as an argument between Mom and Dad). You get the idea. Insightful parents are discerning.

Insightful Parents Practice Patience

We've devoted an entire chapter in this book to becoming a patient parent. But when we talk about wisdom and insight, we need to revisit this quality. As Augustine said, "Patience is the companion of wisdom."

Allow us to give you an example of the kind of patience we're talking about by letting our friend and colleague Henry Cloud tell you about his childhood:

> When I was four years old, I came down with a leg disease that left me bedridden, then in a wheelchair, and then in braces and on crutches for two years. I went overnight from a very active child to one with a serious disability. My doctor told my parents it was imperative they make me do things for myself and not spoil my character by doing everything for me.
>
> I remember an incident at church when my parents were making me go up a long flight of stairs on my crutches. I was struggling and taking a long time, but they were prodding me on. I stumbled, got redirected, and continued on one slow step after another. I'm sure it was painful to watch.
>
> Suddenly, from behind us I heard a woman say to her husband, "Can you believe those parents are making that child do that?"
>
> I don't remember what my parents said, but years later I wondered how my mother did it. One of the most caring people I

> Like an ability or a muscle, hearing your inner wisdom is strengthened by doing it.
>
> **Robbie Gass**

know, she is also one of the most care-taking, the kind who has difficulty making the dog go outside in the rain. I can only imagine what it was like for her to let a crippled child struggle through things she could have helped with.[7]

The instinct of every caring parent would be to help a child who was struggling in such a way, but Henry's parents had the insight to resist their impulse, hold on to patience, and allow their son to do what would be best for him in the long run.

Think about the way patience plays into your desire to be an insightful parent. Are you too quick to solve your child's problems, break up a sibling squabble, or come to the rescue in a lonely social setting? Sometimes the wisest intervention in children's lives involves patiently "giving it time" so they become empowered to find resolution on their own. Remember, "love is patient" — and you can't embody wisdom and insight without plenty of patience.

Insightful Parents Reveal the Folly of Consumerism

When you think of being an insightful parent, managing the message of consumerism may not be the first thing that pops into your head, but it deserves serious attention nonetheless.

Kids have a lot more money than they used to. They are also exposed to a great deal more advertising, not only in front of the television and computer at home, but even at school, through Channel One. As a result, children as young as eighteen months can identify a brand, and their desires influence how adults spend billions of dollars.

> There is no wisdom without love.
> **N. Sri Ram**

Research has shown that children between the ages of two and five cannot differentiate between regular TV programming and commercials. Young children are especially vulnerable to misleading advertising and don't begin to understand that advertisements aren't always true until they're eight.

Psychiatrist Juliet Schor, author of *Born to Buy: The Commercialized Child and the New Consumer Culture*, has discovered that kids' involvement with the consumer culture leads them into more conflict with parents. It also contributes to anxiety, illness, and depression in some children. Schor explains that commercialized children are "more likely to have poor self-esteem, which is not a surprise because a lot of the messages consumer culture sends them are that you're nobody if you don't have the right tennis shoes or you're not drinking the right soft drink."[8]

> Mistakes are lessons of wisdom. The past cannot be changed. The future is yet in your power.
>
> **Hugh White**

Insightful parents recognize the importance of protecting kids from invasive marketing. In her book on modern family life, *The Shelter of Each Other*, author Mary Pipher shares her concern that our consumer culture may be breeding feelings of "narcissism, entitlement and dissatisfaction" in today's kids. Children's identities shouldn't be defined by their consumer habits. Yet if wise parents don't temper the message from Madison Avenue, that's bound to become the main way children see themselves reflected in the media — as consumers with a distorted self-image and values.

Insightful Parents Eat Humble Pie

One day I (Leslie) found my seven-year-old trying to give his two-year-old brother a drink of milk from his cup. Jackson's clothes were soaked, and I scolded my older son for his carelessness. "Why did you do that, John?" I snapped. John started to answer, but I interrupted: "Jackson can't drink this kind of milk, and look at the mess you've made!"

Ten minutes later, after changing Jackson's clothes, it dawned on me that John had simply been trying to share his milk with his little brother. But because I'd spoken on impulse, his generosity only earned him criticism.

I knew I needed to apologize. "I'm sorry, John," I told him. "I shouldn't have scolded you when you were being so nice to share." His look of relief told me I'd done the right thing.

No matter how much we love our children, we still make mistakes, misjudge situations, and sometimes lose our temper. But insightful parents are humble enough to own up to their mistakes and apologize when necessary. As parents, we may fear that if we admit we were wrong, our authority will be undermined. And when we fail, we often find it easier to ignore our shortcomings than to acknowledge that we've goofed.

The truth is, offering an honest apology shows integrity and respect and encourages our children to do the same when they make mistakes. "It is so important for an adult to apologize because it shows the child it's okay to make mistakes and say you are sorry," says Dr. John Gottman. "When you say, 'I shouldn't have done that,' your child will have a rock-solid sense that her feelings matter to the people who are most important in her life."[9]

Insightful parents know that apologizing doesn't undermine authority. It bolsters it. An honest apology won't automatically undo the damage, of course, but it will help restore your relationship with your child. An apology instantly lowers defenses and communicates, "I want to listen." And as Oliver Wendell Holmes said, "It is the province of knowledge to speak and it is the privilege of wisdom to listen."

Insightful Parents Are Grounded

Actor Jimmy Stewart found comfort in Psalm 91. When the United States entered World War II in 1941, Stewart enlisted in the Army

Air Corps and prepared to go overseas. Stewart's father, Alex, choked up when he tried to bid farewell to his son, so he wrote a note for Jimmy to read en route. After being shipped out, Jimmy read the words his father had been unable to say aloud:

My dear Jim boy,

Soon after you read this letter, you will be on your way to the worst sort of danger. Jim, I'm banking on the enclosed copy of the 91st Psalm. The thing that takes the place of fear and worry is the promise of these words. I am staking my faith in these words. I feel sure that God will lead you through this mad experience. I can say no more. I only continue to pray. Goodbye, my dear. God bless you and keep you. I love you more than I can tell you.

Dad

As a veteran of the Spanish-American War, Alex Stewart knew the comforting power of Psalm 91:3–5 for those preparing for battle: "Surely he will save you from the fowler's snare.... You will not fear the terror of night, nor the arrow that flies by day."

Jimmy Stewart returned home a decorated war hero, unharmed even though his record included twenty combat missions. During the height of battle, Stewart said he learned to lean on the words of his tattered copy of Psalm 91, especially verses 1 and 2, which speak of God as a refuge and fortress. Upon returning home, he told his father, "What a promise for an airman. I placed in his hands the squadron I would be leading. And, as the psalmist promised, I felt myself borne up."

Jimmy felt borne up because his father had passed on grounded wisdom. Insightful parents understand the value of being grounded in the Bible, God's Word. The Bible is the sacred book of Christians, and we view it as timeless, relevant, comforting, authoritative, and divine. It takes precedence over tradition, creeds, churches, philosophy, and psychology. It isn't subject to the fluctuating tides of human thought. God's Word gives parents solid footing.

Of course, insightful parents realize the Bible can be misused. Its authority can be misdirected and manipulated. But like Alex Stewart, a parent can never go wrong when accessing God's Word to comfort and guide a child.

> Face your deficiencies and acknowledge them; but do not let them master you. Let them teach you patience, sweetness, insight.
>
> **Helen Keller**

For Discussion

1. On a scale of 1 to 10, how would you rank the importance of being an insightful parent? Why?

2. On that same scale, how would you rank your natural inclination to instill wisdom in your child?

3. In specific terms, when are you most likely to demonstrate the qualities of insight, as noted in this chapter, with your child? Name the times or conditions.

4. When is the next time you are likely to have an opportunity to demonstrate insight with your child? What can you do now to maximize the opportunity?

CHAPTER 13

Practicing the Presence of God: Are You a *Prayerful* Parent?

Religious words have value to the child only as experience in the home gives them meaning.
John Drescher

It started when John was six. He skinned his knee a bit while trying to ride a new bike and began to wail with pain. His bawling went far beyond what the little accident deserved, so Les, the ever-creative psychologist, attempted to distract John by looking at his scrape and singing that goofy song: "You put de lime in de coconut, you shake it all up ... and you say, 'Doctor!'"

John immediately converted his cry into laughter. It was genius. I looked at Les with a big grin, and he winked back at me as we picked up the bike and brushed off our son so he could try riding again.

The little ritual has become a habit in our home. Singing that song when John's tears are more for drama than from pain has spun us out of some intense situations more than once. What we didn't realize was how carefully Jackson, our three-year-old, was paying attention.

That became abundantly clear when Les was tucking the boys into bed recently. I was outside their bedroom door listening in as Les debriefed their day and initiated their nighttime prayers.

John had had a particularly tough day in his first grade class, and Les prayed that tomorrow would go much better. But when it came time for Jackson to pray, he took a different angle: "Dear Jesus, thank

> Prayer — secret,
> fervent, believing
> prayer — lies at the
> root of all personal
> godliness.
>
> **William Carey**

you for Mommy and Daddy ... and help Johnny to put de lime in de coconut."

Les and John snickered while Jack just kept on praying. He didn't see the humor. He just knew he wanted his "big bubby" to feel better.

Few things are as precious as a child's prayers. As one person has put it, "Though her voice is small and mild, all heaven stills for the prayer of a child." Every prayerful parent understands that when it comes to practicing the presence of God, our children can teach us as much as we teach them.

Look up the word *prayerful*, and you'll see that it means "inclined or given to praying." The definition also might include the word "devout." We can discover the full meaning of the word by studying its use in Scripture.

The word *prayer* occurs about eighty-five times in the New Testament. In the Greek, the term conveys the idea of an offering that is brought with a request to God. In the King James Version, it is translated with the old word "beseech" and has to do with intensity. In other words, in prayer we cry out to God, "Abba, Father" — literally "Daddy."[1]

A prayerful person, one who talks and listens to our heavenly Father, exudes a sense of reverence and grace. As Ole Hallesby, a pioneer in theological education, said, "To pray is nothing more involved than to lie in the sunshine of God's grace." A prayerful parent is grace-filled. The point is that prayer can permeate a parent's personality. It compels us to be the parents God wants us to be.

The Undeniable Importance of Being a Prayerful Parent

According to *Newsweek*, "81 percent of mothers and 78 percent of fathers say they plan eventually to send their young child to Sunday school or some other kind of religious training."[2] Most parents sincerely want to raise children who are empathic, know right from wrong, and attempt to follow the Golden Rule. Of course, it's comforting to know that so many of us make moral values a priority in our parenting. But prayerful parenting goes even deeper than instilling moral values. Prayerful parents provide a spiritual underpinning to their kids' lives that is more important to them than you might imagine. Why? Because children are often more spiritually attuned and sensitive to practicing the presence of God than we are.

If any adult ever understood this, surely it was C. S. Lewis. Less than one month before he died in 1963, Lewis wrote the following letter to a young girl who wanted to know if any other books in the Chronicles of Narnia series were going to be produced. It turned out to be a fond and fitting farewell to all of his devoted readers.

Dear Ruth,

Many thanks for your kind letter, and it was very good of you to write and tell me that you like my books; and what a very good letter you write for your age!

> There is hardly ever a complete silence in our soul. God is whispering to us well nigh incessantly.
>
> **Frederick W. Faber**

If you continue to love Jesus, nothing much can go wrong with you, and I hope that you may always do so. I'm so thankful that you realized the "hidden story" in the Narnia books. It is odd, children nearly always do, grown-ups . . . hardly ever.

I'm afraid the Narnia series has come to an end, and am sorry to tell you that you can expect no more. God bless you.

Yours sincerely,
C. S. Lewis[3]

As we've said, children, more than we know, have a connection to God that we don't always recognize. Another example of this truth that underscores the importance of being a prayerful parent is the story of a little girl named Schia.

When Schia was four years old, her baby brother was born. Little Schia began to ask her parents to leave her alone with the new baby. They worried that, like most four-year-olds, she might want to hit or shake him, so they told her no. Over time, though, since Schia wasn't showing signs of jealousy, they changed their minds and decided to let Schia have her private conference with the baby.

> Parenthood calls for faith of the most radical sort.
>
> **Elizabeth Cody Newenhuyse**

Elated, Schia went into the baby's room and shut the door, but it opened a crack—enough for her curious parents to peek in and listen. They saw little Schia walk quietly up to her baby brother, put her face close to his, and say, "Baby, tell me what God feels like. I'm starting to forget."[4]

As we grow older, we lose some of our heartstrings—the ones that tie us to God. Life becomes more cluttered, and if we aren't intentional, we soon forget what God feels like. That's precisely why prayerful parents devote special attention to practicing the presence of God with their children.

A Self-Test: How Prayerful Are You?

The following true/false self-test is designed to get your wheels turning. Don't worry about trying to get the "right" answer; just give the answer that lines up with what you currently believe.

T   F   Prayer is one area where it's best to teach a child how to pray, rather than model being prayerful.

T   F   If children learn to pray correctly, they can expect all their prayers to be answered in the way they would like.

T   F   As long as a child regularly attends church, he'll automatically pick up on the meaning of prayer at home.

T   F   Prayer is primarily a private matter between the person praying and God.

T   F   A child's prayers are relatively meaningless until they become more mature.

Scoring: If you answered "true" to any of these five items, you will benefit from brushing up on how to be a prayerful parent. Even if you answered "false" to each of these items, you can always learn new ways to become more prayerful.

How to Become a Prayerful Parent

According to the latest survey from the Barna Research Group, about two out of three parents of children under age twelve attend religious services at least once a month and generally take their children with them.[5] However, the survey of 1,010 adults found that most parents have no plan for the spiritual development of their children and have little or no training in how to nurture a child's faith.

In other words, most parents are willing to let their church provide all of their children's spiritual training. But not prayerful parents. While they may place high value on what the church can provide for their child, they know that practicing the presence of God at home requires far more than what the church can offer.

So what do prayerful parents do? Let's take a look.

Prayerful Parents Teach Their Children How to Hear God

"What do you think God is saying to you, Jackson?" We asked our three-year-old this question during a recent car trip after he told us that he prayed God would bring him some new toys.

Jackson was quiet for a moment and then said, "I think he's going to call you."

It's tough for a little one to understand how God communicates with us, isn't it? As a three-year-old, our son half expects God to ring us up on the phone. But truth be told, we can help children of any age tune their ears to God's voice. We just need to let them know what his voice sounds like.

For example, we can teach our kids how to listen to that small inner voice. We can teach them that God sometimes speaks through other people. The Bible tells us that Jesus was "moved with compassion" for people. This compassion is one of the clearest indications that God is talking to us. What else does the voice of God sound like? How do you experience his voice? It's an important question to answer, because your child needs your help to understand.

Consider the boy whose father leans over during a symphony orchestra concert and whispers to him, "Listen for the flutes in this song. Don't they sound beautiful?" The child, unable to distinguish the flutes, looks up at his father quizzically. "What flutes, Father?"

The child needs to learn what flutes sound like on their own, separate from the rest of the orchestra, before he is able to hear them in a symphony. So it is when we listen for God. Unless we teach our children to hear God's voice in the quiet moments of life, they will not be able to hear God in the symphony sounds of life.

So when God speaks to you, consider letting your child in on the conversation. Explain to your child that prayer is more than talking; it's also listening.

> God never ceases to speak to us, but the noise of the world without and the tumult of our passions within bewilder us and prevent us from listening to Him.
>
> **François Fénelon**

Prayerful Parents Talk about What They Believe

We tend to believe that actions speak louder than words. But according to a recent study by Purdue University, words are just as mighty as deeds when it comes to passing on our religious beliefs to our children. The study, which appeared in a recent issue of the *Journal of Applied Developmental Psychology*, found that children were more likely to adopt their parents' beliefs when they had a clear understanding of what the parents believed.[6]

This means that if you want your child to embrace a relationship with God through prayer, you not only need to pray but also need to talk about prayer and why it matters. You not only need to attend church but also need to talk about why church is important. Lynn Okagaki, who conducted the study, is a professor of child development and family studies at Purdue. She queried fifty-eight female students and thirty-six male students between the ages of eighteen and twenty-five. "We found the accuracy of a child's perception of a parent's beliefs is affected by all of the things that a parent does," she explains. Such things, for example, include taking the time to explain our beliefs and encouraging our kids to participate in activities that we think support those beliefs.

No wonder Moses instructed the Israelites to talk about the Ten Commandments with their children when they got up in the morning, as they went about their daily routines, and when they went to bed at night. In contrast to the popular proverb, actions don't necessarily speak louder than words. Not only do we need to walk our walk; we need to talk about it as well.

Prayerful Parents Teach
Their Children to Pray

The rote prayers we use to introduce our kids to communicating with God are catchy. Saying, "God is great, God is good," before diving into a plate of spaghetti or reciting, "Now I lay me down to sleep ..." while getting tucked into bed is fine, but even young children can learn how to talk to God about more than eating and sleeping.

Greg Asimakoupoulos, father of three daughters and pastor of a church not far from our home in Seattle, has had tremendous influence on how we've been teaching our children to pray. You may have heard of the ACTS—Adoration, Confession, Thanksgiving, and Supplication—method of prayer. Of course, it's far too complicated for young children. After all, the words *adoration, confession, thanksgiving,* and *supplication* aren't part of their vocabulary. But Greg showed us how each of these four categories relates to a phrase with which our children are quite familiar—phrases we want our children to use in everyday conversation.

I love you. Adoration is nothing more than telling God we love him. Kids know what it means to express love to those they care about. For children, communicating love is a natural response to feeling loved. So we need to help our little ones see the many ways God shows his love to them. When we help our kids understand how much God loves them, they'll be more inclined to express their love to him.

I'm sorry. Children aren't capable of understanding the theological basis and consequences of confession and absolution, but they sure do know what it means to say, "I'm sorry." We can tell our children that God wants to hear the feelings of our hearts. And he wants to offer forgiveness when we say, "I'm sorry." Of course, we don't want to pressure our kids to confess simply for confession's sake. But teaching them that a simple "sorry prayer" is appropriate will help them learn that God is a forgiving God.

Thank you. Saying, "Thank you," is typically the most natural part of a prayer for a child. "Thank you, God, for Mommy and Daddy ..." is a common way for our little ones to begin their nighttime prayers. But we don't want this little phrase to lose its meaning in their minds. We encourage you to set up your prayer time with your children by first talking about what they appreciated during their day. This practice can help them say a prayer of thanksgiving that's more than mere habit.

Please. The S in the ACTS prayer acronym stands for *supplication*. It's just a fancy word that refers to respectfully asking a favor—the operative word being *respectfully*. The supplication part of a prayer isn't a flagrant wish list; it's a time to "ask, seek, and knock" for what we believe we need. Jesus, after all, challenged his disciples to think of themselves as children who readily ask their heavenly Father for the necessities of life. So teach your kids to say "please" to God. They can ask for everything from the courage to stand up to the schoolyard bully to a healthy recovery for a grandfather who's had heart surgery. Kids need to know God wants them to approach him with their hearts' desires.

Prayerful Parents Acknowledge Answered Prayers

Denise Boone of Littleton, Colorado, tells about her eight-year-old son, Jonathan, who plays on a hockey team. One day his coach announced a contest. The winner would receive two tickets to a Colorado Avalanche National Hockey League game. The Boones' son competed hard, but the tickets went to another boy.

159

On the drive home, young Jonathan shed tears of disappointment. Denise told him, "If the desire of your heart is to go to an Avalanche game, you should pray about it."

She explained to Jonathan that God isn't like Santa Claus and doesn't give us everything we want, but that we should tell him our desires and leave them in his hands. At bedtime that night, Jonathan made his request known to God.

"God, this is Jonathan.... I'd like to go to an Avalanche game. I know you are busy with a lot of other things, but I'd really like that."

Denise's husband didn't know about their son's prayer, but the next day he came home from work and announced that a friend had given him tickets to watch the Avalanche practice. It wasn't a game, but Jonathan was excited.

The practice was held at the Pepsi Center in downtown Denver. Their seats were just eight rows up from the glass surrounding the ice, right above the players' bench. Seeing that some boys were standing by the glass, Jonathan went down and joined them. Thrilled to be so close, he watched his favorite player, legendary goalie Patrick Roy, at work.

Suddenly Roy skated over to the bench. He had broken the blade on his hockey stick. As the trainer handed him a new stick, Roy looked at Jonathan and pointed. The trainer took the broken stick and handed it over the glass to Jonathan. He was elated. He held the stick above his head as if he had won the Stanley Cup.

> Earth's crammed with heaven,
> And every common bush afire with God;
> But only he who sees takes off his shoes —
> The rest sit round it and pluck blackberries.
>
> **Elizabeth Barrett Browning**

Patrick Roy's stick now hangs on Jonathan's bedroom wall, but it's more than just a souvenir. As Denise says, "It reminds our son of God's goodness."

Of course, God doesn't always answer our prayers the way we'd like, but every prayerful parent knows how important it is to acknowledge his answers whatever they might be.

Prayerful Parents Are Content with God's Answers

Our son John, in kindergarten, was having a tough time with a little boy in his class. John wanted to be friends with the boy, but the boy wasn't treating him kindly. He ignored John and didn't include him in conversations and play-time activities. So one morning as I (Leslie) drove John to school, John and I prayed about the situation. We asked God to help John find a way to connect with the boy so that they might become friends. John and I both prayed out loud as I drove.

When I picked John up at the end of the school day, the first thing I asked him was, "How did it go with your friend?" I was hoping and expecting that God would have answered our prayers in some way that would increase John's faith.

John's response: "It didn't go so well. He ignored me and didn't play with me. He didn't even talk to me."

Feeling devastated for him and worried about how this incident might impact his faith, I was almost afraid to probe further, but I did: "John, how does that make you feel when we prayed about it all the way to school this morning and it didn't turn out the way we hoped?"

John was quiet for a moment. Then he said, "Well, Mom, I guess God said, 'Next time.'"

Despite the fact that John didn't get the answer to his prayers that he had hoped for, his faith wasn't broken. He still felt God's loving presence in his life, just as he still feels his parents' loving presence even when his father or I say, "Next time."

For Discussion

1. On a scale of 1 to 10, how would you rank the importance of being a prayerful parent? Why?

2. On that same scale, how would you rank your natural inclination to practice the presence of God with your child?

3. In specific terms, when are you most likely to demonstrate spiritual awareness and prayerfulness with your child? Name the times or conditions.

4. When is the next time you are likely to have an opportunity to demonstrate spiritual sensitivity with your child? What can you do now to maximize the opportunity?

PART THREE

BECOMING THE PARENT YOU WANT TO BE

CHAPTER 14

Steering Clear of the Parent You Don't Want to Be

If it was going to be easy to raise kids,
it never would have started with something called labor.
Anonymous

Two ministerial students from Samford University in Birmingham, Alabama, were doing summer evangelistic work in a rural area near Montgomery. One hot day they stopped their car in front of a farmhouse and proceeded up the path through a gauntlet of screaming children and barking dogs. When they knocked on the screen door, the woman of the house stopped her scrubbing over a tub and washboard, brushed back her hair, wiped perspiration from her brow, and asked them what they wanted.

"We would like to tell you how to obtain eternal life," one student answered.

The tired homemaker hesitated for a moment and then replied, "Thank you, but I don't believe I could stand it."

Let's face it, parenting can be tough work, and in those especially grueling moments, we sometimes wonder how we can make it — let alone be the parents we want to be.

These are the times when we need to take special care to avoid being the parents we *don't* want to be. Have you ever thought of that? All of us — no matter how well we parent at our peak — have weary moments, moments when we are infused with fatigue or worry that can cause us to do and say things we quickly regret. These are moments when we not only fail to measure up to our best but come dangerously close to being our worst.

We All Have "Smudges"

In the widely read book *Tuesdays with Morrie*, Mitch Albom writes, "All parents damage their children. It cannot be helped. Youth, like pristine glass, absorbs the prints of its handlers. Some parents smudge, others crack, a few shatter childhoods completely into jagged little pieces, beyond repair."[1]

You wouldn't be reading this book if you were a parent who falls into this last category, but if you're like most good-intentioned parents, you have smudged or will smudge the glass of your child's life. Of course, that's exactly what life is. Nobody makes it through childhood spotless. We all have smudges. Our goal as parents, is to keep those smudges to a minimum. And one of the best ways to do just that is to become fully aware of when we are likely to handle our children carelessly.

> My father was a Methodist and believed in the laying on of hands, and believe me, he *really* laid them on!
>
> **A. W. Tozer**

Do you know the signs that warn you're about to do or say something as a parent that you'll regret? I (Les) recognize these signs when I'm feeling pressured by a project, on task, hungry, and frustrated by something one of my sons is doing. Those factors have proven to be a bad combination for me. And that's precisely when I'm prone to be the parent I don't want to be.

Who Hijacked My Brain?

In the Dark Ages, a time of superstition, ignorance, and religious fanaticism, the majority of Europe's population lived in fear of werewolves — mystical beings thought to be humans with the ability to transform themselves into half-man – half-wolf beasts that roamed the countryside eating their victims during a full moon.

Ever since then, people have been fascinated by these mythical creatures. Hollywood made its first movie about them in 1913. Dozens of others have followed. Numerous television shows and novels have centered on werewolves as well. Commentators say our fascination with the fictional creature is due to the polarity of personalities within one person. There's something about this schism that most of us identify with.

Of course, even more dramatic than the stories of werewolves is Robert Louis Stevenson's book *The Strange Case of Dr. Jekyll and Mr. Hyde*, one of the most widely known and referenced stories on the planet. Soon after its publication in 1886, the book was being quoted in pulpits and publications around the world. Dozens of major stage and film adaptations followed. It is now solidly implanted in popular culture. The very phrase "Jekyll and Hyde" has become shorthand to mean bipolar behavior.

Why do you think these stories are so enduring? Surely it has something to do with seeing a bit of ourselves in these dramatic characters. We've all experienced a snap that reveals our dark side and

> When I turned into a parent, I experienced a real and total personality change that slowly shifted back to the "normal" me, yet has not completely vanished.
>
> **Sonia Taitz**

turns us into someone we don't want to be. Neurological researchers have actually pinpointed just where it happens. Deep in our brain is an almond-shaped set of neurons called the amygdala. It forms a part of our limbic system and is responsible for managing emotions and helping us empathize.

> Even when freshly washed and relieved of all obvious confections, children tend to be sticky.
>
> **Fran Lebowitz**

Researchers have also coined a phrase to describe what happens when this part of our brain loses control. They call it an "amygdala hijack." It occurs when your emotions take over without restraint. Since the amygdala is in the most primitive part of the brain, it has been programmed to act fast, bypassing the cortex — the thinking part of the brain. When threatened, it immediately decides to either attack or run for safety. We know this phenomenon as the "fight or flight response," and it happens in a millisecond. Of course, today the threats we experience are mostly symbolic, not physical. As parents, for example, we feel threatened when our child is being irrational or wasting our time. But we are still prone to the same biological response of either fighting or fleeing. That's when we have an amygdala hijack and allow our emotions to get the better of us. That's when we become part of the problem instead of the solution. Later, upon reflection, we realize that what we did was inappropriate or downright wrong.

Getting Your Emotions under Control

The opposite of an amygdala hijack is *emotional intelligence*, the ability to handle feelings so that they are relevant to the situation and so that we react appropriately. Daniel Goleman, who popularized the term through his book on the subject, says, "Emotional Intelligence is a master aptitude, a capacity that profoundly affects all other abilities, either facilitating or interfering with them."[2]

When it comes to parenting, the hallmark of emotional intelligence is the ability to reshape the emotional landscape of a potentially troublesome situation with a child. Thus, humor and empathy are traits that can de-escalate conflict and help you maintain the qualities you want to exhibit. With emotional intelligence, you'll say things like, "I feel upset when you do that," rather than shouting, "You make me crazy!"

Sure, you're thinking, I'd like to keep my emotions under control and maintain the qualities that are important to me, but how? It all comes down to practicing patterns of thinking and behaving that lead to emotional de-escalation. Here's how it works.

First, ask yourself what you are feeling. One school of thought believes "awareness is curative." Once you become aware of your emotions, you can begin to manage them. Sounds elementary, we know, but it's so true. When you're on the verge of losing it because your arms are full of grocery bags and your child is dawdling as she gets out of the car, you will be miles down the road if you can simply say to yourself, "I'm feeling impatient." You'll be amazed at what this momentary self-reflection does to put a clamp on an emotional outburst.

Next, do everything you can to put yourself in your child's shoes. Try to go beyond thinking what they might be thinking to feeling what they might be feeling. The challenge is to put yourself in their skin and see the world as they see it. We won't kid you—seeing life through your child's eyes is no easy task—but it's guaranteed to slow down or stop an emotional hijack. Recently, while parked along a busy road, I (Les) was trying to get both of our boys unloaded so they'd be safe. "John," I said, "I want you to unbuckle yourself and climb out on Jack's side." He protested for no apparent reason: "I don't want to." We went back and forth for a moment, until

> How can one have a sweet fragrance whose father is an onion and whose mother is garlic?
>
> **Arabian proverb**

finally I said, "It doesn't matter what you want — get out on that side!" John started to move, but very slowly. I was about to lose it, but I paused, tried to put myself in his eight-year-old body, and realized that he didn't understand the reasoning behind my instructions. I hadn't explained the safety issue. As soon as I saw the situation from his perspective, my emotions immediately came under control.

Finally, validate your child's emotions. This step requires serious intention. We don't do it automatically. But like empathy, it will almost always de-escalate the emotional heat of a given moment. Instead of saying, "There's no reason to get so upset," when your child gets mad and throws a tantrum because he's unable to put together a puzzle, acknowledge that his reaction is natural. Say, "It's really frustrating when you can't finish a puzzle, isn't it?" Telling him his reaction is inappropriate or excessive will cause his emotions to escalate all the more. "You don't understand!" he'll protest. But identifying and validating his feelings will let him know he's understood.

So there you have it — some practical ways to guard against becoming Mr. Hyde. Before wrapping up this brief chapter, however, we want to leave you with one more practical exercise that will help you install a few guardrails along the road to becoming the parent you want to be.

The Parent You Definitely Don't Want to Be

In part 1 of this book, we told you about the personal parenting retreat we held, just the two of us, at Salish Lodge near Seattle. One portion of our twenty-four-hour experience, however, we haven't told you about yet. It involved making a list of the kind of parents we don't want to be.

For us, compiling this list didn't take long. We simply brainstormed for a few minutes about the qualities neither one of us wanted to embody as a parent. In other words, we listed the traits that we definitely did not want to describe us.

We decided that we don't want to be parents who are ...

- Critical
- Judgmental
- Wishy-washy
- Distracted
- Detached
- Indulgent
- Smothering

- Inconsistent
- Jealous
- Perfectionistic
- Conditional
- Angry
- Needy
- Controlling

Of course, the list could go on and on, but these were the qualities that came to mind most readily. The next thing we did was circle the top two traits to which we're most prone. In other words, we identified the traits that were most likely to become our "Mr. Hyde."

For me, those traits were "indulgent" and "smothering." For Les, they were "distracted" and "critical." How about you? You don't have to use our list. Build your own. What traits do you want to steer clear of in your parenting? What are your top two, the ones you'll need to be especially careful to avoid when you suffer an amygdala hijack?

Pastor Chuck Swindoll says that every family with children is a cross between Grand Central Station and the Indianapolis 500. Comedian Martin Mull says, "Having children is like having a bowling alley installed in your head." Parenting, no matter how you look at it, is tough work. And that's why you see some parents who are normally caring, cooperative, and creative turn into rigid, destructive, and impossible people. If you know your weak spots and practice emotional intelligence, however, you'll minimize the smudges on your child's life — and you'll have secured good insurance against being the parent you don't want to be.

> The great man is he who does not lose his child's heart.
> **Mencius**

For Discussion

1. Do you agree with the point that every parent, no matter how well-intentioned, leaves "smudges" on a child's life? Why or why not?

2. What can you do, in specific terms, to avoid an amygdala hijack? In what circumstances with your child is it most likely to occur? What can you do now to curtail it?

3. What two qualities do you definitely not want to embody as a parent and why?

CHAPTER 15

Your Children Become
Who You Are

*Your children will become what you are;
so be what you want them to be.*
David Bly

"We're both Daddy!" So proclaimed John recently when he and his little brother came into the study where Leslie and I were working on this book. They were both dressed in khaki pants and untucked navy blue polo shirts—exactly what I was wearing that day.

"Look, Daddy, we're just like you," Jackson chimed in. They stood side by side with beaming grins.

On impulse, Leslie picked up the camera, arranged us on the front porch, and snapped shots of the three of us as if we were posing as a trio for the cover of a CD. Looking at the shots now, I think my grin was bigger than theirs!

People often say we look alike. And they're not talking about the way we're dressed. The funny thing is, I can't see it. I catch a glimpse of genetic similarity now and then, but it's tough for me to see how total strangers can see our resemblance so blatantly. Regardless, I do know that these two boys will grow up to be more like me than any other man in their lives—for better or for worse. And you know the same is true for you and your children.

That's why we've written this book. The fact that children grow up to be like their parents is the point of the "ten traits worth

> I have frequently gained my first real insight into the character of parents by studying their children.
>
> **Sir Arthur Conan Doyle**

considering." It's the point of becoming the parent you want to be. After all, parenthood isn't about parents; it's about children and the way that we, as their God-given caretakers, shape who they become.

In this chapter we feel compelled to underscore once more the essential point we made in part 1 of this book: Parenting is more about who you *are* than what you *do*.

Why Your Traits Matter to Your Child

Baseball star Cal Ripken Jr. says the sagest advice he ever received about being a parent came not from any child development expert but from a former Orioles teammate named Tim Hulett. Ripken regards Hulett as "the best dad I've ever known."

In one clubhouse conversation still etched in his memory, Ripken recalls Hulett saying, "Your little ones are a blank tape, constantly running and recording information. Whose information do you want on that tape? Yours or somebody else's?"

Ripken, like every other parent, wants his child's tape to be influenced most by him. And it will be. Every intentional parent sees to that. It's what Dorothy Law Nolte was getting at when she penned the lines of her poem "Children Learn What They Live" in 1954. Here's a small portion of it:

If a child lives with fairness, he learns justice.
If a child lives with security, he learns to have faith.
If a child lives with approval, he learns to like himself.
If a child lives with acceptance, he learns to find love in the world.

The full poem has been published worldwide, translated into ten languages, taught in parenting and teaching courses, distributed in doctors' offices, and printed on posters and calendars. It's easy to see why, isn't it? The poem reminds us to be the kind of parents who embody the qualities we want our children to have.

"If a child sees his parents day in and day out behaving with self-discipline, restraint, dignity and a capacity to order their own lives," said psychiatrist M. Scott Peck, "then the child will come to feel in the deepest fibers of his being that this is the way to live."[1] You get the point. Your traits, the unique combination of traits that you and your spouse weave into the fabric of your home, will forever shape the soul of your child.

> If there is anything we wish to change in the child, we should first examine it and see whether it is something that could better be changed in ourselves.
>
> **Carl Jung**

Each Parent Offers Something Different

Speaking of your unique combination of traits, we want to suggest that you don't focus so much on the parent *you* want to be that you neglect the great value your spouse is bringing to your parenting team. You'll experience great synergy when you recognize each other's contributions.

The film *Love Comes Softly* illustrates this point. The film depicts the story of the strength and spirit of a pioneer woman who is put to the test when she unexpectedly becomes a widow. Unable to care for herself, Marty is forced to marry a man and take care of his daughter in return for safe passage on a wagon train.

In one scene, Marty is exasperated with her dual role as wife to Clark and mother to Missie. Getting to know the young girl has been challenging, and after a difficult confrontation with her, Marty decides she can't fill the role of mother any longer.

"I don't know what I was thinking," Marty says. "I can't stay here."

"Why?" Clark asks.

"Why? That little girl hates me. You were right. She does need a mother. But I am not the right person. She doesn't know it, but she is still grieving."

"That is why you are the right person," Clark says.

"It's just not going well," Marty replies.

"It's going just the way I thought it would," Clark says. "I knew she wouldn't like it at first."

"Then why put her through this?"

"Because I love her. And she needs more than I can give her."

"It seems like an awful lot of trouble to go through for just a few months' lessons and letters and sewing."

"Nothing is a waste of time if it adds to the person that you are," Clark replies. "I'm counting on the fact that knowing you is going to add to the person that Missie will become. I know that you can find a way to get through to her."

"How do you know?"

"Because that's what I prayed for."[2]

Did you catch that line? "I'm counting on the fact that knowing you is going to add to the person that Missie will become." This is the message each of us can give to and receive from our spouse. Parenting is a tag-team effort—each parent's traits offer something of great value to your child. And in the end, your unique combination of traits is the stuff of which your child is made.

For Discussion

1. Knowing that who you are as a parent has a significant influence on the course of your child's life, name the other factors that make significant contributions to the person your child will become (for example, genetics, life circumstances, etc.).

2. If you had to assign a percentage to your own traits in relation to these other influences, what percentage would you assign to your traits and why?

CHAPTER 16

Making Your
Top Traits Stick

*There is nothing more influential in a child's life
than the moral power of quiet example.*
William John Bennett

Eleven miles off the east coast of Scotland, in the North Sea, stands the Bell Rock Lighthouse. It has endured the ferocious onslaught of the North Sea's violent storms since 1811. It rests upon less than one acre of solid rock. That small reef is covered by seawater for twenty hours every day. The builders of the lighthouse, Robert Stevenson and his band of sixty-five skilled artisans, had only four hours each day to chink away the stone and gouge a foundation in the rock. As a result of this painstakingly patient work, the 115-foot-tall lighthouse is still in use today.

In a similar way, parents have a short period of time during which to build their children's lives to withstand the storms of life. As parents, we have to take advantage of the little windows of opportunity we get to carve out a foundation for our children. That's why, in this final chapter, we want to urge you to make a commitment. We want you to review the traits you've studied and selected to develop. We want you to revisit the exercise we asked you to complete in chapter 3, focusing especially on part 4 of the exercise, where you selected two traits that you want to realize more fully as a parent. Are they still the same two you would put at the top of your list now? If not, that's fine.

The point here is to identify your top two traits and then take some practical steps to build them into your character.

Nail Down Your Top Two

We often feel the way Robert Stevenson must have felt while building the Bell Rock Lighthouse. We know the opportunities to be the parents we want to be are fleeting. We know we must take full advantage of the moments that we have to demonstrate the qualities we prize. In our case, the top two for Les are "affirming" and "patient," and the top two for Leslie are "authentic" and "insightful." These are the traits each of us identified as being deficiencies in our personal parenting profile.

You undoubtedly feel the same way we do—wanting to seize every opportunity to improve your parenting. So let us help you make a plan for developing the traits that will help you become the parent you want to be.

First, just as we did, state clearly what two traits you want to embody more. You can write them here in the book for now if you'd like, but eventually you'll find it helpful to write them on a handy note card where you can see them often.

Father's Top Two Traits to Develop:

_____

_____

Mother's Top Two Traits to Develop:

_____

_____

Think through where you can place the note card listing your two traits. You don't necessarily have to see them every day, but you want them to be visible to you on occasion. We ended up putting ours on the inside of our vehicles' sun visors. That way we don't become immune to them, but whenever we pull the visors down to block the sun, we're reminded of the traits we want to develop. As a bonus, it seems to us that it's often in the car—shuffling the kids to and fro—that we need the most reminding of the parents we want to be.

As a quick aside, when we have friends riding with us who happen to see the words *affirming* and *patient* written on the note card, they always ask about the purpose of the card. When we tell them, they invariably say, "That's a great idea. I'm going to do that."

> Oh, what a tangled web do parents weave when they think that their children are naive.
>
> **Ogden Nash**

Once you've clearly stated the two traits you want to develop, you can take several practical actions to be sure they make their way into your being. After all, it's one thing to get inspired to be a better parent; it's quite another to actually become one. The following tips will help you do just that.

Take Inventory

Every so often our family takes a little hike at a big park on Magnolia Bluff in Seattle. It's less than ten minutes from our home, but it feels like a world away. You can hike for miles through the woods, but eventually you'll reach a clearing that overlooks the trails and beyond to Puget Sound. Recently as we stood in this clearing, Jackson, age three, said, "Look how far we came from!" He was pointing to the snowcapped Olympic Mountains miles and miles away. "Not quite," John, age eight, said with a laugh.

181

Jackson may not have had an accurate perspective, but he certainly has the idea. There's something refreshing about standing on a high vantage point and seeing the distance you've traveled. And that certainly applies to your journey of becoming the parent you want to be. So don't forget to take inventory of what you're accomplishing along the way. Plan a spot on the calendar to plant a mile marker and measure your progress.

We take inventory after each boy's birthday celebration, typically after the party guests are gone and we've cleaned up the house and put the boys to bed. When the house is quiet, we review that child's previous year and the kind of parents we have been.

Ask the Big Question

Few would dispute the enormous impact of the Greek philosopher Socrates. In his various dialogues he touched upon virtually every problem that has occupied subsequent philosophers. His teachings have been among the most influential in the history of Western civilization, and his works are counted among the world's finest literature. And if you were to ask anyone in the know to quote him, more often than not, you would hear a simple sentence that has become his trademark: "The unexamined life is not worth living."

Socrates probably didn't have parenting in mind when he said these now famous words so long ago, but they couldn't be more relevant to moms and dads. In the daily blur of activity that sur-

> The hand of the parent writes on the heart of the child the first faint characters which time deepens into strength so that nothing can efface them.
> **R. Hill**

rounds most homes, self-examination, the kind requiring serious soul-searching, is precious and rare.

So here's what we do to make sure we don't live "unexamined lives" as parents. We ask each other, from time to time, what we've come to call the "big question." It goes like this: If I'm working at being more patient, I'll ask Leslie, "How am I doing at being a patient parent?" Amazingly, she almost always has an answer!

Truthfully, we've found this kind of questioning to be a very helpful practice for keeping our top two traits in play. When one of us asks the other the big question, we'll eventually reverse roles so that we're both getting feedback.

By the way, if you're brave, you can ask the same question to your child. Of course, doing so will be meaningful only if your child is an appropriate age. When I recently asked John if he thought I was a patient parent, he said, "I didn't even know you were sick!" John's idea of being "patient" had more to do with being in the hospital than practicing a virtue.

Accept "Good Enough" on Occasion

The late British psychiatrist D. W. Winnicott put forth the idea of "good-enough mothering." He was convinced that mothering could never be perfect because of the mother's own emotional needs. The same applies to fathers. "Good-enough parenting" refers to the imperfect, though adequate, provision of emotional care that can raise a healthy child.

Keeping in mind this idea of "good enough" can go a long way toward making sure your top two traits don't get consumed by perfectionism. After all, you've selected your two traits because they don't come easily for you. These are "deficit traits," so you are bound to mess up on occasion. That's okay. You're still good enough.

Family therapist Jean Brautigam Mills says, "The good-enough parent is all that is really needed to raise children who become normal adjusted adults. Let's start by giving up this 'perfection' business. No one is perfect—not you, and not your child. Mistakes in parenting are opportunities to teach our children [that] when mistakes happen, there is a process whereby we can admit it, know what must be done, and move on to recovery or forgiveness."

What is to be gained by this "good enough" perspective? Well, parents who accept good enough on occasion are bound to be far happier than those seeking perfection. And so are their kids.

Receive Rather Than *Achieve* Your Top Traits

The qualities you seek to exemplify as a parent are sometimes *received* more than they are *achieved*. They are not the fruit of our efforts but the fruit of a life lived in an effort to be more like Christ.

We've found that when we are feeling inadequate as parents—when we've done our level best to be the parents we want to be but still aren't making the mark, God reverses roles. The instant that we feel inadequate and confess our insufficiency to him, we receive what we need.

Like turning water into wine, God turns our best efforts, which too often fall short, into something better than we could have offered on our own. God makes his strength perfect in our weakness. Without God, in other words, we could never be the parents we want to be.

For Discussion

1. When it comes to asking the "big question," what is likely to keep you from doing it? Plan a time right now to discuss with your spouse (and/or your child) how you are doing at fulfilling your top two traits (the two traits you've chosen to develop).

2. What do you make of the final section of this chapter—that you often receive rather than achieve the traits you are working to improve? Does this concept make sense to you? Share an example of a time when God empowered you to demonstrate a parental quality you couldn't have demonstrated on your own.

A Special Word
for Single Parents

Single parenting is arguably one of the most difficult jobs in the world. Whether brought on by death, divorce, or separation, this circumstance leaves a mom or dad to deal single-handedly with traditional aspects of parenting. That's why we could not write this book without including a special note to you as a single parent.

Whether you have already read *The Parent You Want to Be* or have skipped straight to this appendix, we want you to know that we kept you in mind as we were writing every page. While we didn't change our phrasing to stipulate this—primarily because it would have proven too cumbersome to you the reader—we want you to know how deeply we feel what you are going through.

We've counseled numerous single parents and talked with many others in classes and at seminars where we've spoken. And while we haven't been in your shoes, we have carefully studied what it would be like to walk where you walk.

So in this appendix we want to give you some special advice on applying our message to your specific situation.

The Big Picture

Divorce or death ends a marriage but not a family. The family reorganizes itself into what researchers are beginning to call the "binuclear family." This family is a nuclear family divided in two—the hus-band/wife relationship has been dissolved, but not the father/mother, mother/child, or father/child relationship.

According to a recent Census Bureau report, single-parent fam-ilies have displaced two-parent families with children as the most common type of U.S. household. In 1990 there were over 25 mil-lion families with two married parents and children (known as the "nuclear family"). By 2000, however, the number of nuclear families had dropped by almost a half million, and the number of single-adult households had surged past 27 million.*

Single-parent families are the fastest-growing family form in the United States. No other family type has increased in number so rap-idly. And 87 percent of single-parent families are headed by women.

How Single Parenting Is Different

A single-parent family is not the same as a two-parent family with one parent temporarily absent. The permanent absence of one parent dramatically changes the way in which the parenting adult relates to the children. Usually the mother becomes closer and more responsive to her children. Her authority role changes too. A greater distinction between parents and children exists in two-parent homes. Rules are developed by both mothers and fathers. Parents generally have an implicit agreement to back each other up in child-rearing matters and to enforce mutually agreed-on rules.

In the single-parent family, no other partner is available to help maintain such agreements; as a result, the children may find them-selves in a much more egalitarian situation. Consequently, they have more power to negotiate rules. Have you noticed this? Do you some-times feel badgered more as a single parent? Any parent who has tried

---

* Cheryl Wetzstein, "More Homes in U.S. Go Solo," *Washington Times Online* (August 17, 2005), www.washtimes.com.

to get children to do something they don't want to do knows how soon he or she can be worn down. So single parents like yourself are often more willing to compromise or give in. In this way, children acquire considerable decision-making power in single-parent homes. They gain it by default — the single parent, in contrast to a two-parent team, finds it too difficult to argue with them all the time.

On the plus side, children in single-parent homes may learn more responsibility. For example, they may learn to help with kitchen chores, to clean up their messes, or to be more considerate. In single-parent homes, children are encouraged to recognize the work their parent does and the importance of cooperation. Is this true for you? One single mom told us that before the divorce, her husband had always washed the dishes. At that time it had been difficult to get the children to help around the house. Now, she said, the children have learned to pitch in and help with the dishes, vacuuming, and other things that need to be done — otherwise, they wouldn't get done.

Of course, we don't have to tell you that any positives that emerge in a single-parent home are often overshadowed by challenges. A review of relevant studies on children from single-parent households found that these children tend not to do as well academically as those from two-parent families. They are also more likely to drop out of high school. We don't need to highlight all of the challenges that sociologists have devoted volumes to. That isn't our purpose here, and besides, you've already heard them. What we want to do is focus on how you can maximize your parenting situation by focusing on the single parent you want to be.

The Single Parent You Want to Be

Whether you're newly single and hoping to find another soul mate or you're happy and content to parent on your own, we want you to know that the message of this book is as relevant to you as it is to any parent—maybe more so.

Let's face it, life for any family isn't easy. As families navigate the often turbulent waters of life, storms are inevitable. And for some families, those storms bring an unpredictable upheaval that makes it seem, at least for a time, that the course has been lost. If this is how you are feeling, studying the "ten traits worth considering" (outlined in this book) may very well be one of the best ways you can get your parental bearings. And even if you're already navigating the white waters of single parenthood without capsizing, these traits will help you stay the course with deeper intention.

Everything we write about in part 1 of the book applies to you. The only chapter that requires a bit of adaptation is chapter 3: "How to Become the Parent You Want to Be." As you may already know, chapter 3 contains a detailed exercise designed to be discussed with a spouse. Your situation probably makes such a discussion impossible—though if you are divorced or separated, you might want to consider the exercise if your relationship is conducive to it. And if it is, by the way, you are in the minority. Most single parents will need to go this exercise alone, at least to some degree.

Here's what we suggest. Read through the exercise on how you can develop your personal parenting profile and then determine whether it would be valuable to talk through the exercise with someone else. You may find that you gain plenty by simply doing it on your own. However, if you feel you would benefit from some give-and-take, consider going through this exercise with a personal coach, a counselor, or a trusted friend. You may even want to discuss the exercise with another single parent who can identify with your situation. Whatever you choose, don't write off the exercise as irrelevant. You may not be able to work through every question, but you'll quickly see how helpful it is to journal your answers even if another soul never reads a word.

We know you've got a tough job. We know you sometimes feel like you're doing the work of two parents—and you probably are. But don't lose sight of the fact that what you are doing is the most important and meaningful job you will ever have.

Summary Sheet
Worth Noting

We've provided the following summary of the ten traits outlined in this book as a convenient reminder. Feel free to copy it and display it in a location where you'll see it from time to time. You'll also find a convenient PDF file of this summary sheet at our website (www. RealRelationships.com) for easy printing.

Ten Traits Worth Considering

- Giving the Praise They Crave: Are You an *Affirming* Parent?
  Realistically praise what your child does, and show him that you notice, love, and value him.

- Counting to Ten—Again: Are You a *Patient* Parent?
  When frustrated, stay calm and cool and try to see the world from your child's viewpoint.

- Hearing What They Don't Say: Are You an *Attentive* Parent?
  Listen for the feelings, values, and fears your child does not overtly express and find gentle and meaningful ways to let her know you understand.

- Seeing a Picture of Their Future: Are You a *Visionary* Parent?
  Treat your child's dreams seriously and foster a future that will help him actualize what he aspires to do and be.

- Building a Better Bond: Are You a *Connected* Parent?
  Create bonding experiences by intentionally fostering activities you both enjoy together.

- Commemorating Milestones: Are You a *Celebratory* Parent?
  Communicate a powerful message of love to your child by planning festivities to commemorate developmental signposts worth remembering.

- Keeping Your Word: Are You an *Authentic* Parent?
  Use everyday occurrences to "walk your talk" and show your child that you are deserving of her trust.

- Creating the Safest Place on Earth: Are You a *Comforting* Parent?
  Instill deep emotional security in your child by maintaining a non-anxious presence and reassuring him that you are always available to talk.

- Instilling Wisdom: Are You an *Insightful* Parent?
  Become an "emotional coach" for your child by accepting negative emotions as a fact of life and using them as opportunities to teach life lessons.

- Practicing the Presence of God: Are You a *Prayerful* Parent?
  Use opportune times to talk to God together with your child and discuss ways you can pray for each other.

Notes

CHAPTER 3
How to Become the Parent You Want to Be:
An Exercise

1. Richard Louv, *Childhood's Future* (New York: Anchor, 1991).

CHAPTER 4
Giving the Praise They Crave: Are
You an *Affirming* Parent?

1. Garrison Keillor, *We Are Still Married* (New York: Penguin, 1990).

2. Leah Yarrow, "Adults Get a 'D' for Being Disconnected from Kids," *Chicago Tribune* (March 18, 2001).

3. Josh Tyrangiel, "The Art of Being a Confidence Man," *Time* (October 18, 2004).

4. Haim G. Ginott, *Between Parent and Child* (New York: Avon, 1965), 47.

5. Calvin Tompkins, "Profiles: The Creative Situation," *New Yorker* (January 7, 1967), 23. Quoted at www.wildestcolts.com/parenting/morequotes.html.

CHAPTER 5
Counting to Ten — Again:
Are You a *Patient* Parent?

1. J. Strayer and W. Roberts, "Empathy and Observed Anger and Aggression in Five-Year-Olds," *Social Development* 13 (2004): 11.

2. Jon Kabat-Zinn, *Everyday Blessings: The Inner Work of Mindful Parenting* (New York: MJF Books, 2000).

CHAPTER 6
Hearing What They Don't Say:
Are You an *Attentive* Parent?

1. Helmut Thielicke, *How to Believe Again*, trans. H. George Anderson (Philadelphia: Fortress Press, 1972).

2. "Eminem," www.answers.com/topic/eminem.

CHAPTER 7
Seeing a Picture of Their Future:
Are You a *Visionary* Parent?

1. Gary Smalley and John Trent, *The Blessing* (New York: Pocket, 1990).

CHAPTER 8
Building a Better Bond:
Are You a *Connected* Parent?

1. Nick Stinnet, Nancy Stinnett, Joe Beam, and Alice Beam, *Fantastic Families* (West Monroe, La.: Howard Publishing, 1999), 13.

2. National Center on Addiction and Substance Abuse at Columbia University, www.casacolumbia.org/absolutenm/templates/Home.aspx.

3. Quoted in June Fletcher, "The Dysfunctional Family House," *Wall Street Journal* (March 26, 2004), W1, W8.

4. Matthew 5:7 MSG.

5. Karl E. Miller, "Are Family Meals Good for the Health of Adolescents?" *American Family Physician* 71, no. 6 (March 15, 2005).

CHAPTER 9
Commemorating Milestones:
Are You a *Celebratory* Parent?

1. StrategyOne poll of 1,000 adults (November 9 – 11, 2001).

2. "Marriage Partnership," *Contemporary Christian Music* 10, no. 2.

3. John McCrone, *The Ape That Spoke: Language and the Evolution of the Human Mind* (New York: Avon, 1992), 17.

4. Marianne Neifert, www.dr-mom.com.

CHAPTER 10
Keeping Your Word:
Are You an *Authentic* Parent?

1. Quoted in John Ashcroft, *Lessons from a Father to His Sons* (Nashville: Thomas Nelson, 1998), 44.
2. Quoted in *Servant* (Summer 1998), 9.
3. John Trent, *Be There!* (Colorado Springs: Waterbrook, 2000).

CHAPTER 11
Creating the Safest Place on Earth:
Are You a *Comforting* Parent?

1. Zeynep Beringin, *Raising a Secure Child* (New York: Penguin, 2004).
2. www.msnbc.com (December 29, 2003).
3. Helen Fisher, *Anatomy of Love* (New York: Ballantine, 1994).
4. Quoted in Ruth Schenk, "I Choose You," *Southeast Outlook* (February 24, 2005).

CHAPTER 12
Instilling Wisdom:
Are You an *Insightful* Parent?

1. *Stepmom*, DVD, directed by Chris Columbus (Los Angeles: Sony Pictures, 1999).
2. Proverbs 4:5–10.
3. John Gottman, "Effects on Marriage of a Psycho-Communicative-Educational Intervention with Couples Undergoing the Transition to Parenthood," *Journal of Family Communication* 5 (2005): 1–24.
4. Robert Fulghum, *All I Really Need to Know I Learned in Kindergarten* (New York: Ivy Books, 1989).
5. Matthew 18:3 MSG.
6. Corrie ten Boom, *The Hiding Place* (New York: Random House, 1982).
7. Henry Cloud, *How People Grow* (Grand Rapids: Zondervan, 2001).
8. Quoted in Andrea Sachs, "Junk Culture," *Time* (October 4, 2004).
9. John Gottman, "Effects on Marriage of a Psycho-Communicative-Educational Intervention with Couples Undergoing the Transition to Parenthood," *Journal of Family Communications* 5 (2005): 1–24.

CHAPTER 13
Practicing the Presence of God:
Are You a *Prayerful* Parent?

1. Romans 8:15; Galatians 4:6.

2. Karen Springen, "Raising a Moral Child," special issue, *Newsweek* (Winter 2000), 71.

3. Christin Ditchfield, "Straight out of Narnia," *Today's Christian* (Nov/Dec 2005), 32.

4. *Leadership* 16, no. 3.

5. "Parents Do Little about Kids' Faith Training," *Southeast Outlook* (May 22, 2003).

6. L. Okagaki, K. A. Hammond, L. Seamon, "Socialization of Religious Beliefs," *Journal of Applied Developmental Psychology*, no. 2 (1999): 20.

CHAPTER 14
Steering Clear of the Parent You Don't Want to Be

1. Mitch Albom, *Tuesdays with Morrie* (New York: Hyperion, 2003), 104.

2. Daniel Goleman, *Emotional Intelligence: Why It Can Matter More Than IQ* (New York: Bantam, 1997).

CHAPTER 15
Your Children Become Who You Are

1. M. Scott Peck, *The Road Less Traveled: A New Psychology of Love, Traditional Values and Spiritual Growth* (New York: Touchstone, 1998).

2. *Love Comes Softly*, DVD, directed by Michael Landon Jr. (Los Angeles: 20th Century Fox, 2004).

Look for Les and Leslie's
companion DVD series for

THE
PARENT
YOU WANT TO BE

Interested in hosting the Parrotts for one of their highly acclaimed seminars? It's easy. Just visit *www.RealRelationships.com* to learn more and complete a speaking request form.

Les and Leslie speak to thousands in dozens of cities annually. They are entertaining, thought-provoking, and immeasurably practical. One minute you'll be laughing and the next you'll sit still in silence as they open your eyes to how you can make your relationship all it's meant to be.

"I've personally benefited from the Parrotts' seminar. You can't afford to miss it."

Gary Smalley

"Les and Leslie's seminars can make the difference between you having winning relationships and disagreeable ones."

Zig Ziglar

"The Parrotts will revolutionize your relationships."

Josh McDowell

"Without a doubt, Les and Leslie are the best at what they do and they will help you become a success where it counts most."

John C. Maxwell

Learn more about the Parrotts'
"Becoming Soul Mates Seminar."

*Click on www.RealRelationships.com
to bring them to your community.*

Your Time-Starved Marriage

How to Stay Connected at the Speed of Life

Drs. Les and Leslie Parrott

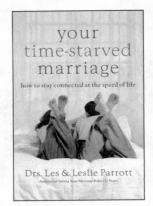

This is not a book about being more productive — it's a book about being more connected as a couple. In *Your Time-Starved Marriage*, Drs. Les and Leslie Parrott show how you can create a more fulfilling relationship with time — and with each other.

The moments you miss together are gone forever. Irreplaceable. And yet, until now, there has not been a single book for couples on how to better manage and reclaim this priceless resource. The Parrotts show you how to take back the time you've been missing together — and maximize the moments you already have. *Your Time-Starved Marriage* shows you how to:

- relate to time in a new way as a couple
- understand the two lies every time-starved couple so easily believes
- slay the "busyness" giant that threatens your relationship
- integrate your time-style with a step-by-step approach that helps you make more time together
- stop the "time bandits" that steal your minutes
- maximize mealtime, money time, and leisure time
- reclaim all the free time you've been throwing away

Learn to manage your time together more than it manages you. Dramatically improve your ability to reclaim the moments you've been missing. *Your Time-Starved Marriage* gives you tools to feed your time-starved relationship, allowing you to maximize the moments you have together and enjoy them more.

Hardcover, Jacketed   0-310-24597-4

Also Available:

0-310-81053-1	Time Together	Hardcover, Jacketed
0-310-26885-0	Your Time-Starved Marriage	Audio CD, Unabridged
0-310-27103-7	Your Time-Starved Marriage Groupware DVD	DVD
0-310-27155-X	Your Time-Starved Marriage Workbook for Men	Softcover
0-310-26729-3	Your Time-Starved Marriage Workbook for Women	Softcover

Love Talk

Speak Each Other's Language Like You Never Have Before

Drs. Les and Leslie Parrott

A breakthrough discovery in communication for transforming love relationships.

Over and over, couples consistently name "improved communication" as the greatest need in their relationships. *Love Talk*—by acclaimed relationship experts Drs. Les and Leslie Parrott—is a deep yet simple plan full of new insights that will revolutionize communication in love relationships.

The first steps to improving this single most important factor in any marriage or love relationship are to identify your fear factors and determine your personal communication styles, and then learn how the two of you can best interact. In this no-nonsense book, "psycho-babble" is translated into easy-to-understand language that clearly teaches you what you need to do—and not do—for speaking each other's language like you never have before.

Love Talk includes:

- The Love Talk Indicator, a free personalized online assessment (a $30.00 value) to help you determine your unique talk style
- The Secret to Emotional Connection
- Charts and sample conversations
- The most important conversation you'll ever have
- A short course on Communication 101
- Appendix on Practical Help for the "Silent Partner"

Two softcover "his and hers" workbooks are full of lively exercises and enlightening self-tests that help couples apply what they are learning about communication directly to their relationships.

Hardcover, Jacketed   0-310-24596-6

Also Available:

0-310-80381-0	Just the Two of Us	Hardcover, Jacketed
0-310-26214-3	Love Talk	Audio CD, Abridged
0-310-26467-7	Love Talk Curriculum Kit	DVD
0-310-81047-7	Love Talk Starters	Mass Market
0-310-26212-7	Love Talk Workbook for Men	Softcover
0-310-26213-5	Love Talk Workbook for Women	Softcover

Relationships

An Open and Honest Guide to Making Bad Relationships Better and Good Relationships Great

Drs. Les and Leslie Parrott

Drs. Les and Leslie Parrott understand first-hand our deep need for relationships; and as relationship experts, they know what it takes to build strong, lasting bonds. In *Relationships*, the Parrotts take us below the surface to the depths of human interactions — to the nitty-gritty realities, the ups and downs of building vital, satisfying connections. They provide the tools needed to handle tough times and to really succeed at forging strong, rewarding relationships with friends, with the opposite sex, with family, and with God.

The Parrotts share not just from their knowledge, but from their hearts and lives to help us all understand:

- who we are and what we bring to our relationships
- how our families of origin shape the way we relate to others
- how to relate to God without feeling phony ... and much more.

Filled with insightful, true-life stories and thought-provoking questions, *Relationships* is an honest and timely guide to forming the rich relationships that are life's greatest treasure. This book is accompanied by a workbook that contains more than 35 self-tests to help you put what you learn into action. The *Relationships Workbook* will help you internalize cutting-edge strategies, skills, and insights for nurturing healthy relationships.

Hardcover, Jacketed   0-310-20755-X

Also Available:

0-310-22466-7	Relationships	Groupware, Adult
0-310-24266-5	Relationships	Softcover
0-310-22473-X	Relationships Leader's Guide	Softcover
0-310-22585-X	Relationships Participant's Guide	Softcover
0-310-22438-1	Relationships Workbook	Softcover

Pick up a copy today at your favorite bookstore!

I Love You More

How Everyday Problems Can Strengthen Your Marriage

Drs. Les and Leslie Parrott

How to make the thorns in your marriage come up roses.

The big and little annoyances in your marriage are actually opportunities to deepen your love for each other. Relationship experts and award-winning authors Les and Leslie Parrott believe that your personal quirks and differences—where you squeeze the toothpaste tube, how you handle money—can actually help draw you together provided you handle them correctly.

Turn your marriage's prickly issues into opportunities to love each other more as you learn how to:

- build intimacy while respecting personal space
- tap the power of a positive marriage attitude
- replace boredom with fun, irritability with patience, busyness with time together, debt with a team approach to your finances ... and much, much more.

Plus—get an inside look at the very soul of your marriage, and how connecting with God can connect you to each other in ways you never dreamed.

Softcover   0-310-25738-7

Also Available:

0-310-26582-7	I Love You More Curriculum Kit	DVD
0-310-26275-5	I Love You More Workbook for Men	Softcover
0-310-26276-3	I Love You More Workbook for Women	Softcover

Pick up a copy today at your favorite bookstore!

You Matter More Than You Think

What a Woman Needs to Know about the Difference She Makes

Dr. Leslie Parrott

Am I making a difference?
Does my life matter?

"How can I make a difference when some days I can't even find my keys?" asks award-winning author Leslie Parrott. "I've never been accused of being methodical, orderly, or linear. So when it came to considering my years on this planet, I did so without a sharpened pencil and a pad of paper. Instead, I walked along Discovery Beach, just a few minutes from our home in Seattle.

"Strange, though. All I seemed to ever bring home from my walks on the beach were little pieces of sea glass. Finding these random pieces eventually became a fixation. And, strangely, with each piece I collected, I felt a sense of calm. What could this mean? What was I to discover from this unintentional collection?"

In this poignant and vulnerable book, Leslie shows you how each hodgepodge piece of your life, no matter how haphazard, represents a part of what you do and who you are. While on the surface, none of these pieces may seem to make a terribly dramatic impact, Leslie will show you how they are your life and how when they are collected into a jar—a loving human heart—they become a treasure.

Hardcover, Jacketed   0-310-24598-2

Saving Your Marriage Before It Starts

Seven Questions to Ask Before—and After—You Marry

Drs. Les and Leslie Parrott

A trusted marriage resource for engaged and newlywed couples is now expanded and updated.

With more than 500,000 copies in print, *Saving Your Marriage Before It Starts* has become the gold standard for helping today's engaged and newlywed couples build a solid foundation for lifelong love. Trusted relationship experts Drs. Les and Leslie Parrott offer seven time-tested questions to help couples debunk the myths of marriage, bridge the gender gap, fight a good fight, and join their spirits for a rock-solid marriage.

This expanded and updated edition of *Saving Your Marriage Before It Starts* has been honed by ten years of feedback, professional experience, research, and insight, making this tried-and-true resource better than ever. Specifically designed to meet the needs of today's couples, this book equips readers for a lifelong marriage before it even starts.

The men's and women's workbooks include self-tests and exercises sure to bring about personal insight and help you apply what you learn. The seven-session DVD features the Parrotts' lively presentation as well as real-life couples, making this a tool you can use "right out of the box." Two additional sessions for second marriages are also included. The unabridged audio CD is read by the authors.

The Curriculum Kit includes DVD with Leader's Guide, hardcover book, workbooks for men and women, and *Saving Your Second Marriage Before It Starts* workbooks for men and women. All components, except for DVD, are also sold separately.

Curriculum Kit   0-310-27180-0

Also Available:

0-310-26210-0	Saving Your Marriage Before It Starts	Audio CD, Unabridged
0-310-26565-7	Saving Your Marriage Before It Starts Workbook for Men	Softcover
0-310-26564-9	Saving Your Marriage Before It Starts Workbook for Women	Softcover
0-310-27585-7	Saving Your Second Marriage Before It Starts Workbook for Women	Softcover
0-310-27584-9	Saving Your Second Marriage Before It Starts Workbook for Men	Softcover

3 Seconds
The Power of Thinking Twice

Les Parrott, PhD

Just three seconds. The time it takes to make a decision. That's all that lies between settling for "Whatever" ... or insisting on "Whatever it takes."

3 Seconds shows how to unleash the inner resources that can move you to a whole new level of success. It comes down to six predictable impulses that most of us automatically accept without a second thought. You can replace them with new impulses that lead toward impact and significance. For instance, it takes *Three Seconds* to ...

Disown Your Helplessness: The First Impulse: "There's nothing I can do about it." The Second Impulse: "I can't do everything, but I can do something."

Quit Stewing and Start Doing: The First Impulse: "Someday I'm going to do that." The Second Impulse: "I'm diving in ... starting today."

Fuel Your Passion: The First Impulse: "I'll do what happens to come my way." The Second Impulse: "I'll do what I'm designed to do."

Inhale ... exhale ... the difference of your lifetime can begin in the space of a single breath. The decision is yours. Start today.

Hardcover, Jacketed   0-310-27249-1

Pick up a copy today at your favorite bookstore!

**ZONDERVAN**
.com